# Saving St Teilo's

Bringing a medieval church to life

0190

32

First published in 2009 by
Amgueddfa Cymru – National Museum Wales,
Cathays Park, Cardiff, CF10 3NP, Wales.
www.museumwales.ac.uk

© The National Museum of Wales

ISBN 978 0 7200 0598 1

Editing and production: Mari Gordon
Design: mopublications.com
Print: Gomer Press

Available in Welsh as *Achub Eglwys Sant Teilo: ailgodi adeilad canoloesol*,
ISBN 978 0 7200 0599 8

Previous page: A reconstruction of the celebration of Sunday mass, showing the elevation of the host by
the priest. The main server holds the edge of his chasuble in one hand and a taper in the other, while
two more servers in the foreground kneel in prayer, one holding a thurible for incense. Also present are
two singers and two lay members of a guild, the latter holding tapers. Mass could also be celebrated
with just one server, often on weekdays (Low Mass), and with deacon and subdeacon, when they were
available, often on Sundays and greater feasts (High Mass). *Artist: Mark T. James*

# Saving St Teilo's

Bringing a medieval church to life

EDITED BY GERALLT D. NASH

NATIONAL MUSEUM WALES BOOKS 2009

# Contents

# Entrada
## In the beginning

## Introduction

The opening of Llandeilo Tal-y-bont Church has filled a long-felt gap at St Fagans. By now, more than forty buildings have been re-erected, after being dismantled and removed from their original locations and brought to the Museum, where they inform and engage many hundreds of thousands of people every year. But it might not be obvious to visitors that the re-erection of buildings at St Fagans has always operated under two golden rules.

Firstly, the Museum is more interested in the common or typical, rather than in the unique. This relates to all levels of society, and can encompass a typical manor-house as much as a typical cottage. Crucially, there is no place at St Fagans for architectural one-offs. Buildings are chosen for the story they tell, rather than for any intrinsic aesthetic merit they might have. It is always a happy coincidence when the two things come together. Each re-erected building at St Fagans is therefore representative of more than itself, and is important because of the contribution of that building-type to society in all its diversity.

Secondly, only buildings with little or no hope of being saved in-situ are accepted for re-erection. By today, some buildings might be the only things that have survived reasonably intact from the time they were built. Their contemporary historic environment might have changed – woods will have shrunk or expanded, field-boundaries changed, neighbouring buildings demolished or, conversely, a formerly isolated structure might have been swallowed by modern urban development; in other words, the building itself might, by now, be out of context with its original setting. Nevertheless, that is where it has always been, and it still contributes to the sense of place. Occasionally, however, some buildings are threatened with dereliction or even demolition, and in these cases the Museum may be able to offer an alternative that will preserve them for future generations.

Following the first of these rules, the Museum had long been keen to acquire a typical parish church. Representing religion in Wales falls within St Fagans's wide remit, and clearly that has meant, at the very least, acquiring both a church and a nonconformist chapel. Capel Pen-rhiw, a late-eighteenth-century Unitarian chapel from west Wales, was opened to the public in 1956,

which made the need for a church all the more pressing. Even though the Museum was offered churches in its early days – Llanrhychwyn, high in the hills above the Conwy valley, being a notable example – none fully met the requirements.

Throughout the 1970s and 1980s, more and more Welsh religious buildings were becoming redundant, through declining congregations and growing maintenance costs. The Museum was offered four churches during this period – some impossibly large and unrepresentative, others no more than roofless ruins. But St Teilo's Church from Llandeilo Tal-y-bont seemed to meet the criteria. It was no longer required for worship, and was a burden on the Church in Wales. Its future, at best, was to be turned into a managed ruin, and even that seemed problematic as its condition rapidly deteriorated.

To the Museum at the time, the great virtues of St Teilo's seemed to be that it had barely been touched by the Victorian or later restorers, and, given that its early nineteenth-century fittings had been destroyed, offered the possibility of being restored to its medieval or early post-medieval appearance. Also, intriguingly, its crumbling plaster appeared to conceal extensive traces of early wall paintings.

And so it proved.

**Eurwyn Wiliam**
Deputy Director General, Amgueddfa Cymru – National Museum Wales

# Who was Teilo?

Teilo was an important religious leader who lived in south Wales during the sixth century. He was born in Penally, south Pembrokeshire about AD 500, and was a contemporary of Dewi (St David). Both are said to have been taught by the learned scholar Paulinus at Whitland in west Wales. It is claimed that he travelled to Rome with Dewi and Padarn, where they were received by the Pope. Teilo established a religious community at Llandeilo Fawr in Carmarthenshire, and his influence soon spread throughout south Wales. In AD 547 a plague swept across Britain devastating the population and livestock. Teilo and his followers fled to Cornwall, and thence to northern Brittany, where they were received by Samson, Bishop of Dol (originally from Llantwit Major).

Later, they moved west in search of land on which they could settle. The local landowner, the Count of Kastel Gall, agreed to give them as much land as Teilo could mark out between dusk and dawn. On the appointed evening, as he was about to set out, a stag appeared by his side, which he mounted and rode away to claim his land. The Count, fearing that he would lose too much of his territory, set his hunting dogs on him, but Teilo escaped and took shelter in an oak tree. Eventually the dogs became tired and returned to their owner, enabling Teilo to continue, the stag having, miraculously, reappeared.

After seven years and seven months the plague ended and Teilo returned to Wales to continue his Christian ministry. However his death, in about AD 580, created another problem: Penally, his birthplace, Llandeilo Fawr, where he established his first church and Llandaff, who claimed him as their bishop, all wished to have his body for burial. The various parties could not agree, but decided to sleep on the matter overnight and pray for guidance. When they re-convened the following morning they found that the body had miraculously triplicated itself, so that everyone was satisfied.

Teilo became a popular saint during the Middle Ages with at least thirty churches being dedicated to him in south Wales and another seven in Brittany, where the *troménie* of St Teilo, an ancient procession of his relics around the parish, is still performed in the village of Landeleau to this day. He is usually depicted dressed as a bishop holding a crozier in his left hand and seated on a stag.

The story of Teilo's life can now be seen on the Church's rood loft. It depicts the most popular legends about the saint, all hand-carved from a single solid piece of oak. St Teilo's day is celebrated on 9 February. He is the patron saint of horses and apple trees.

(Left) The statue of St Teilo, carved in oak by Emyr Hughes and based on surviving medieval statues in Brittany. A statue of the saint to whom a church was dedicated was generally displayed alongside the high altar.

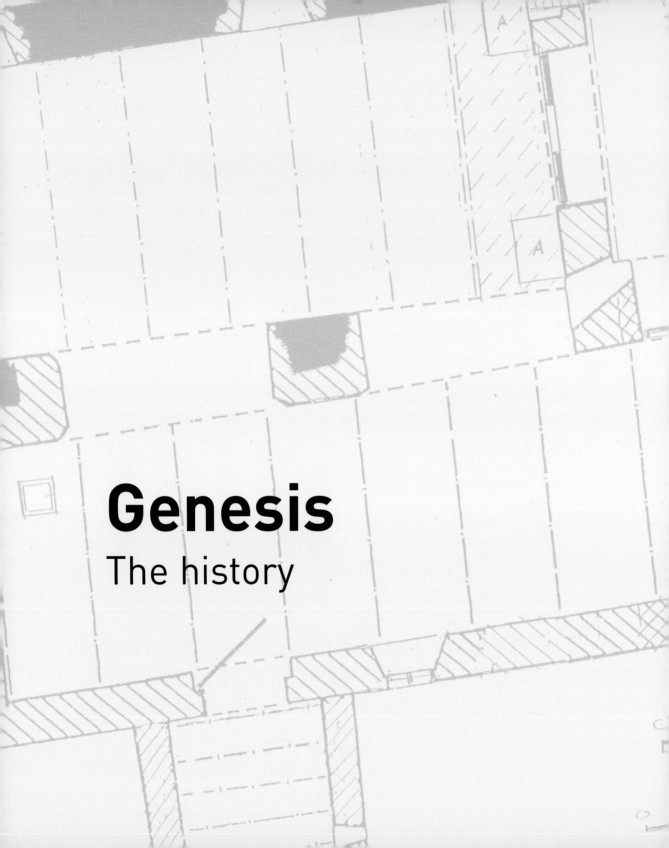

# Genesis

## The history

## The first church

How far back does the church's history stretch? A number of sources can be examined. Written sources include records, such as the Welsh annals and charters, and narrative sources, such as saints' lives. Archaeological clues include concentrations of early medieval inscribed stones or stone sculpture, and types of burial or field monuments such as cemetery enclosures. Unmarked sites can also be suggested by place-names: '-llan' means 'enclosure' and 'merthyr', coming from the Latin martyrium, 'martyr's grave'.

Confirmation of a pre-Norman church beside a crossing point of the River Loughor at Llandeilo Tal-y-bont has for many years been based on charter references preserved in the Book of Llandaf. Several of these refer to Llandeilo Tal-y-bont, either as villam sancti teliaui de talipont or Lan Teliau Talypont, one of four places in Glamorgan named after St Teilo that are mentioned. According to charter 140 dated about AD 655, 'King Meurig and his wife Onbraust ... returned Lan Teliau Talypont to bishop Euddogwy' (Oudoceus), who signed as summus episcopus. The bounds of the large estate of about 4,000 acres are defined as stretching from the river Loughor to the source of the Camffrwd and thence to the Dulais, a distance of about three miles.

The first archaeological evidence for the existence of a precursor to the surviving stone church came to light in 1999, during the sorting of wall rubble in the initial stages of the reconstruction programme. Within the rock pile lay a short pillar of fine-grained sandstone, with incised designs on one face. Examination of these has revealed at least two phases of stone cutting. The first stage involved pecking a simple linear Latin cross and two smaller equal-armed crosses with dots in their interspaces. Many such cross-carved stones may have marked graves, though some may have functioned differently – demarcating land as Christian estate, or serving as foci of worship. Incised crosses are widespread in Wales, and are difficult to date. On the basis of the simple cross form and the proportions of the stone, and comparison with examples from Glamorgan and Carmarthenshire, a seventh- to ninth-century date is possible. The second stage involved someone modifying the central area of the cross by incorporating it into a half-round shield motif, leaving the extremities of the cross projecting above and below. The spaces above the cross arm were decorated with five drilled dots, as in a dice. Similar motifs occur on stones from Carmarthenshire, Radnorshire and Pembrokeshire. A shield-shaped ('quasi-heraldic') motif also occurs on a stone from St Dogmaels in Pembrokeshire, although this example has the form of a jousting shield usually dated to the fifteenth century. Half-round shields appear on the Continent from the thirteenth

(Previous page) Sidney and Olwen Webb (the church's main caretakers for some 40 years until the late 60s) with friends, photographed outside the church around 1960. *Courtesy of Bronwen Webb*

The incised stone cross found among the masonry of St Teilo's church, dating from 7th-9th century.

century, and the Llandeilo Tal-y-bont example could date from this period. Later, the stone could have been incorporated into a floor mosaic, as a tile, if it was no longer being used as a pillar stone or marker.

Apart from the porch, which was probably late fifteenth- or early sixteenth-century, and the end of the chancel, which was rebuilt in 1927, those walls of the church that were bonded with lime mortar date from the thirteenth to the late fifteenth century. It seems likely, therefore, that the stone had been incorporated in the church fabric as building material by about AD 1500.

## The church in its medieval setting

Today a visitor to the former site of St Teilo's Church on the east bank of the Afon Llwchwr – the River Loughor – can look downstream and perhaps feel that the whole world is passing by on the busy M4 motorway or the London Paddington to Milford rail line. Yet within the limewashed walls of the churchyard there can be a sense of time standing still. The isolation was commented upon by its vicar, Thomas Clarke, in 1851, as 'most awkwardly situated on the verge of the Afon Llwchwr, surrounded by vast Marches, which are often overflown by Tides and floods...'.

That sensation of timelessness, or even the desire to step back in time to a medieval world, can dominate the reflective mind. The floodplain surrounds the church enclosure, its summer pasture perhaps little changed from the Middle Ages. Isolated beside the river, our church served a dispersed community whose medieval farmed landscape is now camouflaged by field enclosures and eroded by modern farming practices.

One, still visible, medieval monument acts as catalyst in this 'what was it like here then?' enquiry. It is likely that the most prominent feature in the built landscape of around 1200, and contemporary with the early, rectangular masonry church, was the motte and bailey castle a kilometre away. Variously referred to as Talybont Castle, Banc y Rhyfel, Banc Llwyn Domen and even Roman Hill, it was typical of its time. By today, the motte remains as a prominence, but the bailey-bank is ploughed out. Crop-mark photographs reveal two rectangular buildings in the bailey on the south side of the mound. A 1353 reference to *Villa de Talband in qua sunt unum castrum* suggests a stone castle, though no masonry is visible today. Located on the upper edge of rising ground to the south-east of our church, its site commands an exceptional, three hundred and sixty degree-view of the valley. Almost invading the motte is the current harbinger of change – the motorway – as it sweeps down to the river crossing.

North of the church in the neck of a pronounced river meander stands another motte, known as Ystum Enlli. The western feature, also known as Banc Llwyn Domen, is a motte located at a ford. There are no strong historical records of these west bank castles.

The key to the medieval cultural landscape is transport links – by sea, river and land. The territorial boundaries were controlled and reinforced by these former castles, while the River Loughor was the boundary that separated the territory of Carnwyllion from the Gower.

In a Papal Bull of 1119-31 our site is referred to as *Lan Teiliau talypont*. The earl of Warwick, Henry de Beaumont (d. 1119), had already secured Gower for the Normans and he granted the fees of Talybont to Henry de Villers. It is likely that it was he who founded Talybont Castle, the east bank castle, around 1115.

A century later, Talybont Castle was in flames, attacked and destroyed by Rhys Ieuanc and Llywelyn ab Iorwerth. The native princes made frequent incursions into this newly occupied frontier land. From then the castle had another name – Castell Du ('Black Castle').

The missing link in the medieval map is a river crossing. There is a reference to a ford at Ystum Enlli, while a bridge, Pontaberdulais, demolished in the 1940s, is regarded as being fourteenth century. Were there other crossings? According to one recent authority on the Roman road network, two thousand years ago the *Leuca* (Loughor) was crossed at Hendy by the *Via Maritima*, while the main river crossing, by ferry, was at Loughor, protected by a coastal fort and harbour.

From this Roman road system, we can see the medieval succession. The Port Way follows the Roman road and becomes the 'essential artery for Norman incursion and conquest', a conquest that brought with it the first stone church at Tal-y-bont, and another, new way of life for the native community.

## Evidence below ground

The twelfth century witnessed an explosion in church building in Wales, with the reconstruction of timber buildings in stone. If you had travelled through Wales during the first half of the century, you would have seen a land that 'glittered with lime-washed churches, like the firmament with stars' according to the famous panegyric to Gruffydd ap Cynan (d. 1137).

In July 1998 archaeological excavations were undertaken on the footings of the church, in order to answer a number of key questions about its early form and development. It had not been at all clear from the standing architecture whether the east wall of the chancel, rebuilt in 1927, lay on the precise line of the early sixteenth-century east end of the church, or whether there was any evidence for a smaller (or longer) chancel. The team also wanted to establish the precise nature of the wall foundations at different periods, and whether there had been an earlier transept at the east end of the south aisle.

This archaeological project brought staff from the Museum together with local volunteers and students from the University of Wales, Gorseinon College, Morriston Comprehensive School and the present incumbent of St Teilo's in Pontarddulais, the Reverend John Walters. Before excavation began, the Clark Laboratory of London made a geophysical survey of areas within the churchyard, using ground-penetrating radar. This detected burials in all four of the areas surveyed, as well as a number of anomalies within the church that could have been related to structural activity. Augering (boring holes to collect earth samples) around the site confirmed that the raised ground was a natural formation in a floodplain that had experienced migration of the main river channel.

A detailed understanding of the building fabric – such as the walls, mortar and foundations – is an essential part of any comprehensive investigation of a church's development. For churches still in use, only fleeting glimpses of the hidden fabric can be provided as opportunities arise. As St Teilo's Church had already been dismantled, an unrestricted opportunity was provided to clean, record and interpret the entire building through its wall-stubs, which remained in place at ground level. A detailed, stone-by-stone plan was produced, and three small 'keyhole' trenches were excavated inside. It had been thought that the latest addition was a small chapel on the north side of the chancel, known in recent times as the Gronow Chapel. However, interpretation of the wall-stub data significantly modified the phasing of the church's structural history.

An archaeological excavation of part of the south wall in July 1998 revealed a straight joint where the south chapel had been extended to form an aisle during the late 15th century.

No structural evidence for a pre-Norman church was found, but this was not expected, in view of the limited scale of the excavations. The earliest recognisable building phase comprised a simple rectangular nave and chancel of dry-stone construction, built of rounded river boulders and split rubble blocks. To this was added a north and south transept, probably during the fourteenth or early fifteenth century (though not necessarily at the same time), built of thin split rubble and lime mortar. The aisle was added in the late fifteenth century to provide for an expanding congregation, and it is possible that the north chapel was modified or rebuilt at this date. Finally, a porch was added to the south side of the aisle.

## The medieval church and society

It isn't easy for those who live in a largely secular society to imagine the centrality of the parish church in medieval times. Many sources, literary and historical, show how intertwined religion was with every aspect of life. The church was usually the largest and most significant building in most villages, towns and cities. It formed the greatest single investment of most communities, its scale, beauty and colour being in sharp contrast with most surrounding buildings.

In medieval times the church was part of every aspect of life, from birth to death. The church provided care for the poor and the sick. Bishops were considerable personages, often acting as ministers of state and also owning large estates. Indeed the church, and particularly the monasteries, administered a great number of estates and tracts of agricultural land. It has been estimated that the Cistercians controlled around ten per cent of the land in Wales. The monasteries were, however, often good landlords and they and the parishes looked after their poor.

Agriculture was under divine patronage. On Plough Monday, just after Christmas, the plough was blessed. In the spring the priest led his people around the fields to ensure the fertility of the crops, and on 1 August, Lammas, thanksgiving was offered for the harvest.

The year revolved around religious festivals. The celebration of special saints' days, with their ales and festivities, and many other holy days, meant a welcome break from servile labour for all. In the countryside, one of the most hated aspects of Henry VIII's reforms was his abolition in 1536 of a great number of holidays. The year began with the Feast of our Lady on 25 March – a practice recalled by our financial year. The need for redemption and forgiveness was associated with annual confession at Lent for the whole village, and often with penitential – but also often enjoyable – activities such as pilgrimages.

Small groups of parishioners and individuals (as well as, in larger churches, church guilds and societies) sponsored altars, church plate and vestments, and this was the case with even the poorest churches like St Teilo's. Processions and mystery plays gave opportunities for different groups, ranks and professions in society to express their faith and demonstrate their standing. The huge cult of masses for the departed was also inextricably linked with wealth and endowment, not least through chantries.

Medieval church life right up until the sixteenth century was a fascinating blend of the sacred and secular, which might be hard for us to imagine today.

Churches were not just for congregational use. Normally the building would have stood open day and night, and members of the local community would have habitually 'dropped in' for private prayer. Any journey by land or sea could be hazardous, so prayer before the image of St Christopher, the protector of travellers, would be made before undertaking it. In a riverside church close to the sea like St Teilo's, those travelling by boat, or whose livelihood depended on the sea, would also pray before the image of St Nicholas, patron of sailors. In a time when sickness was all too common, prayer would be offered to St Roche, and women in pregnancy would offer a prayer to St Margaret for a safe delivery. Those who had perhaps made a vow or adopted a Rule of Life would come regularly into church; maybe, for example, a group would come at nightfall to sing the *Salve Regina* (Hail Holy Queen) before the statue of the Blessed Virgin Mary.

The building was not only used for worship. Being the most secure and substantial building in the community, it was also the place for meetings and discussion of business, for inquests, for the safe-keeping of valuables and documents, and, if the parish priest had sufficient education himself, for the teaching and nurturing of the young, especially boys being prepared for the ordained ministry or religious life. The church was inextricably bound up with every aspect of life, and our current distinctions, which we take for granted, between sacred and secular, between religion and everyday life, would have had little if any meaning at all for our medieval ancestors.


## Medieval worship

Worship in the early sixteenth century differed considerably from that of this century and the last, at least in outward form. We are used, for example, to churches being stone on the outside and whitewashed on the inside. In the early 1500s it was much more likely that they would be whitewashed on the outside and highly coloured inside with wall paintings, statues, elaborate wood-carving and stained glass, as well as candles and lamps burning everywhere. If we are used to the austerity of a Welsh non-conformist chapel it might strike us more like a Tibetan Buddhist temple than a Christian church, but older Catholics or Orthodox Christians would feel more at home.

As we know from surviving service books, Sunday worship began with morning prayers or Matins, then the blessing and sprinkling of holy water around the church followed by a solemn procession with incense, which would often go round the churchyard. The small choir or parish clerk might then sing the psalms of *Terce* (an office of prayer) while the priest prepared for Mass. Sunday Mass itself would be an elaborate ceremony, conducted mostly in Latin (with a little Greek at the beginning and some Welsh in the middle) with assistants bearing candles, a cross and incense. It differed in some details from both the modern form of Mass and the 'Tridentine Rite'; beginning and ending more simply than the latter, the readings would take place at a lectern close to the people (not at the altar and not from the rood-loft as is sometimes said – except on Palm Sunday). At the offertory (in parish churches) the 'bidding of the bedes' would take place – prayers for all those in need, living and departed. In Welsh-speaking areas, like Llandeilo Tal-y-bont, these prayers would have been in the mother tongue for the most part. Sermons were not always preached, unless the priest was properly licensed, but they would have been in Welsh and sometimes taken from a printed source.

At the heart of the ceremony, bread and wine was taken by the priest and consecrated as the Body of Christ, which he would then lift up high for everyone to see. People would bow or kneel at this 'elevation of the Host' – perceived by all as the most important part of the Mass. A bell would ring so that the whole district could be aware of what was happening and people could kneel even in the fields. Most people would not receive communion (except on special occasions, such as Easter Day) but would take part spiritually by praying the rosary and other prayers as Mass was celebrated, using the wall paintings and decorations to structure their prayers.

On certain days in the year, the ceremonies were different. In Lent and Holy Week, the actions at the altar would be hidden from the people by a large painted curtain hung before the sanctuary, which would not be raised until Palm Sunday. (This practice, and indeed some such painted curtains, can still be found in parts of Germany.) Crosses and statues would also be veiled in a similar way to the great Rood for the whole of Lent, emphasising its character of penance and fasting – indeed, no meat was eaten throughout the season (until, in 1538, Henry VIII allowed the eating of white meat).

Holy Week saw some particularly dramatic services. When Palm Sunday came, two processions, one with the Cross and flowers and branches and one with the Blessed Sacrament, would meet at the churchyard cross, and young boys would represent the

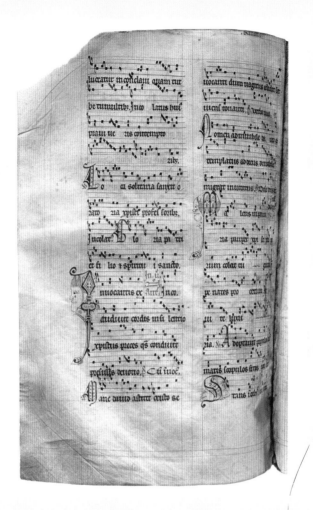

The Penpont Antiphonal is a rare survival of mid-14th-century written musical notation, which was used in the diocese of St David's until the 16th century. *By permission of Llyfrgell Genedlaethol Cymru/National Library of Wales.*

'children of Israel', singing from a temporary structure near the door of the church. Then, on entry to the church, the great Lenten veil would be lifted and the chant *Ave Rex noster* (Hail, our King) sung. On Maundy Thursday, instead of the modern evening Mass, there would be a morning Mass, followed by the church being 'stripped bare', with the removal of altar cloths and washing of all the altars. On Good Friday, many Old Testament readings were chanted and the people crept on their knees to a cross, set up for them to venerate and kiss. The Blessed Sacrament would be taken from its 'hanging pyx' high above the altar and, with the Cross, wrapped in linen and placed in a symbolic 'tomb' in the chancel – the 'Easter Sepulchre'. The Easter Eve Mass would be celebrated the following morning, and there was a beautiful ceremony early on Easter Day when the Cross was solemnly 'raised' and processed around church as the chant *Christus Resurgens* (Christ Rising) was sung and all the bells were rung.

Christmas differed in several respects from our church worship today. There were no Christmas trees, of course, and Gregorian chant was used instead of Christmas carols. Some carols were sung, however, at various related celebrations in the parish both in the home and outside, and these sometimes took the form of dances. By the fifteenth century carols such as *Lullay my liking, Adam lay ybounden* and *The Conventry Carol* became part of a form of drama that grew up around the crib. Welsh carols such as *Ar fore dydd Nadolig* ('On Christmas morning') might well have been used similarly. After the Reformation, many such carols reappeared, slightly altered, in the *Plygain* (dawn) services on Christmas day.

To balance the great emphasis on fasting during the penitential seasons encouragement was given to feasting at Christmas, Easter and special saints' days. There were many such days, and people were excused from their usual hard work and enjoyed the benefit of the 'parish ales'. St Teilo's Day would certainly have been such a day in our church. Special seasonal foods such as hot cross buns and mince pies trace their origins to the celebrations after Mass at these times of feasting.

Funerals and Requiem Masses also played a big part in people's devotion. Part of the Divine Office (the prayers recited daily by priests and some lay people) would be adapted and sung as a *Dirige* and *Placebo* (named from the first words of the Offices for the Dead – from which our word 'dirge' comes). Mass would be offered on the day of burial but also at many other times, such as anniversaries of the day of death, with relatives often offering a small stipend to support the priest who did so.

All in all, the atmosphere of early sixteenth-century worship in Wales was very different from most Christian worship in Wales today – except perhaps for celebrations of the 'Tridentine Rite' in a neo-Gothic church or of the Byzantine Liturgy in a small Orthodox Church. We should imagine an atmosphere of painted walls, many candles, a sense of mystery and with most of the 'action' occurring in the sanctuary, usually behind a decorated screen at the front of the church. Nonetheless, the people would attend in good numbers and would feel deeply involved with the mystery of what was taking place. Their Christian faith was an integral part of their lives, as we know from many contemporary writers, although their involvement was different to the singing of hymns or saying prayers aloud that we know today. For them, participation meant being there, watching the rituals, joining in the processions and, above all, silent adoration and private prayer.

## Post-Reformation and the new church

The years after 1520 proved a time of immense change for Wales, including the parish church at Llandeilo Tal-y-bont. These were the years of the Reformation settlements of the Tudor Dynasty and the Acts of Union of 1536 and 1543, which annexed Wales to England. It is primarily the Reformation that concerns the story of the old church. The Tudor Reformation seems to have been a lengthy process, involving England, Wales and Ireland, which saw changes under Henry VIII, Edward VI, a brief period of return to Catholicism under Mary Tudor and finally the settlements of Elizabeth I.

Changes in theology led to changes in practice that were both visible and audible. The language of worship was now to be the 'vulgar tongue' – English, later Welsh – instead of Latin. The sermon became the main focus of Sunday worship. Lengthy sermons, of up to two hours, demanded a modicum of comfort for listeners, so pews were introduced. Even though such changes were slow to take effect in parts of Wales, images, carved or painted, were eventually removed, to be either destroyed or painted over. Medieval furnishings were also removed, hence the disappearance of the screen and rood loft from St Teilo's Church.

The church continued to be a religious and social focus for the rural communities of the parish. Fairs were held, legal cases were heard and parishioners still came to be married, baptised and buried. Outwardly there would have been very little change in the appearance of the building, while inside there was an evolving development of furnishing and decoration. This is illustrated in St Teilo's by the two fragments of the Lord's Prayer in Welsh, various Biblical quotes painted in the seventeenth century and the complete scheme of 1715 (the Apostle's Creed, Ten Commandments, Lord's Prayer and Royal Arms, with inscribed Churchwardens' names and painter's mark). There was evidence of further renovation in 1736 and 1810, when the church was refurbished with box pews, a 'three-decker' pulpit and new 'Georgian Gothic' windows.

No survey of post-Reformation religion in Wales can ignore the often turbulent relationship between the established Church and the non-conformist churches. One of the earliest signs of non-conformity in the parish of Llandeilo Tal-y-bont seems to be the summoning of four people to appear before the court of the Archdeacon of Carmarthen in December 1662, the case against them being their refusal to attend worship at the parish church. Around 1712, the first non-conformist chapel in the area was built; it is still standing, and now called Yr Hen Gapel ('the Old Chapel').

*Interior of Old Parish Church, Pontardulais*

The eighteenth century saw the beginning of the Methodist movement in Wales and, as with early non-conformity, its history must be seen as distinct from that in England. Some of the clergymen who served the parish of Llandeilo Tal-y-bont were sympathetic to and supportive of the non-conformists. It is said of one, Edmund Nash Leigh, curate from 1769 to 1812, that he was the greatest friend of the Methodist Revival in Wales.

During this period Dafydd William lived in Llandeilo Fach, the farm adjacent to the old church. He was a teacher in the local circulating school, and became a lay-preacher in the early years of the Methodist movement. It is said that on one stormy night, locked out of the house, having returned late from a Methodist meeting, Dafydd took shelter in the church from the overflowing river. There he found inspiration to pen one of Wales's most famous hymns:

A postcard showing the church's interior, with the box pews and three-decker pulpit installed in 1810. The cast iron window in the chancel was inserted in 1927. *Reproduced from an original Frith & Co postcard*

Yn y dyfroedd mawr a'r tonnau,
nid oes neb a ddeil fy mhen
ond fy Annwyl Briod Iesu
a fu farw ar y pren:
cyfaill yw yn afon angau,
ddeil fy mhen i uwch y don;
golwg arno wna im ganu
yn yr afon ddofon hon.

('In the mighty surging waters
Who shall raise my sinking head,
But the faithful bridegroom Jesus,
Who upon the rood hath bled?
Only friend in death's dark river,
Thou shalt hold me, thou shalt keep;
I shall sing, if I but see thee,
In the river's utmost deep.')

*Translated by the Rev. J. W. Wynne Jones (1848-1928)*

He later joined the Baptist Church, moved to the Vale of Glamorgan and was buried at Croes-y-parc at Peterston-super-Ely, near St Fagans.

In 1851, with industrialisation and ensuing population growth, together with increasing difficulties in accessing the church due to seasonal tides and flooding, a new church was built in Pontarddulais by the vicar, the Reverend Thomas Clarke, and it is thanks to him that the medieval church was preserved from 'Victorianisation'. He also built the first school building in the parish in 1848 and a vicarage in 1854. The new church was intended to replace the old, so it was also dedicated in St Teilo's name and made the parish church.

It seems that regular services stopped being held in the old church after 1861; however, in 1877 some renovations were carried out, at a cost of £91. In 1897 the Reverend William Morgan was appointed Vicar; a monument in the new St Teilo's lists the buildings erected during his incumbency, including St Michael's church in Pontarddulais.

Under his leadership and with the financial help of local farmers, the old church was again renovated, and re-roofed at a cost of £100 in 1901. Services were then held until 1970, on three Sundays a year in June, July and August.

Each autumn the church was boarded up until the following spring, when the interior and exterior were cleaned and whitewashed. Many local people remember helping to clean and decorate the church, these often being social occasions as well as a labour of dedication. For some forty years up until the late 1960s it was Mr Sidney Webb and his wife, Mrs Olwen Webb, who were the church's main caretakers, leading and organizing the annual spring-clean. The popular summer services were attended by parishioners of all denominations, and a remarkable photograph taken on a sunny Sunday in July 1934 testifies to this. The last incumbent to lead a service there, in 1970, was the Reverend W. Cynwyd C. Williams.

The old church, although no longer in regular use, witnessed one last important event in the religious history of Wales. On 18 September 1914, Royal Assent was given to the passing of the Bill to disestablish the Church of England in Wales. The tumultuous events of the war of 1914-18 interrupted this process but, finally, on 31 March 1920, the Church in Wales became a disestablished church, now on an equal footing within Wales with every other church. In 1923 a new diocese was created out of the large diocese of St David's, and the ancient church of Llandeilo Tal-y-bont became one of the churches of the Diocese of Swansea and Brecon.

(Left) Crossing the river Llwchwr in coracles to attend a service in the church, around 1900.

(Right) Lime-washing the church was a communal event, as seen in this picture taken about 1960.

(Right) The Rev. W. Cynwyd C. Williams, vicar of St Teilo's Pontarddulais, the last person to officiate at a service in the church, in 1970. *Courtesy of Pam Waterhouse*

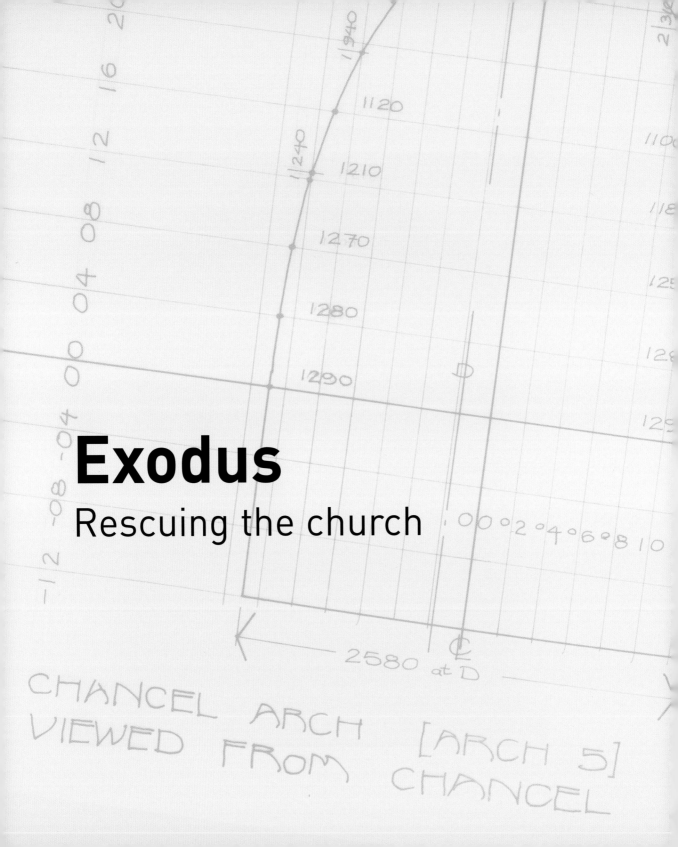

# Exodus
## Rescuing the church

## Recording the structure

When staff from St Fagans first set eyes on the church in 1984, the sight that greeted them was one of sorry decay and dereliction. The windows had been boarded up and ivy had become established over large parts of the outside walls. Most telling was the fact that the roofs had been stripped of their slates and the timbers now stood exposed and vulnerable to the elements. All around were signs of deterioration and vandalism, with several tombs and gravestones broken or pushed over. Inside, things were, if anything, even more depressing. All the early nineteenth-century box pews had disappeared, as had the fine three-decker pulpit and its sound-board and the turned-wood altar rails. No glass remained in any of the windows and the south door had gone. The font lay for-lornly on its side on the floor of the south aisle. We later learned that all the internal fittings and fixtures had been removed to be repaired as part of a government-spon-sored work-creation scheme back in the 1970s, but that they, like the church bell, had mysteriously 'disappeared'!

Some ten years earlier, investigators from the Royal Commission on the Ancient and Historical Monuments of Wales (RCAHMW) had carried out a preliminary survey of the building and noticed what appeared to be traces of pigment or colour on one of the walls. Apparently, rainwater entering the building had loosened a small section of limewash, which had fallen away from the wall. The exposed plaster showed signs of decoration, but quite what it was and when it had been done had to wait until a detailed examination of the walls could be carried out.

In late 1984, a major survey was undertaken, again by RCAHMW, following the decision to move the building to St Fagans. It soon became clear that, with careful detective work and by referring to other, similar, churches in the area, enough evidence remained for St Teilo's to be re-created as it might have looked just before the Reformation. The whole structure, with nave, chancel, chapel, aisle and porch, had all been built by this time, and although most of the carved stone tracery had been taken out from the windows, and features such as the rood loft and screen were missing, it was felt that the Museum's craftsmen could restore it to its former glory. The search for clues began.

Before detailed recording of the building could take place, it was first necessary to remove centuries of accumulated limewash from the outside walls to expose the stonework. This was a slow and painstaking task, carried out using small hand picks.

(Top) The church, photographed in 1984, showing advanced signs of dereliction following the theft of the roof slates.

(Bottom) The south aisle, again photographed in 1984, stripped of all its furnishings and open to the elements. The font can be seen lying on the floor.

During the work, previously hidden details and features came to light, like the outlines of blocked-up windows, straight joints showing where the former west door had been and numerous 'putlog' holes that were once used to support medieval timber scaffolding.

To record the structure, a horizontal 'datum' line was drawn around the walls outside and inside the building. Another line was drawn, at the same level, through the length of the building, extending through the east window in the chancel at one end, and through the partly-blocked nave doorway (now a window) at the other. A second line was then drawn, at right angles to it, across the width of the building. At the point where the two lines crossed, a third, vertical line was drawn. Measurements taken from these datum lines were then used to pinpoint the locations of individual stones, timbers or architectural features.

Starting at the west corner of the nave and working anti-clockwise around the outside of the building, each significant part of the church – every corner, window or door – was given an identification letter, from A to M. Each stone associated with these features was then numbered, so that when measurements were taken they could be recorded and cross-referenced. The numbers were painted onto the stones: external stones were given a white number on a dark grey background, while those identifying internal features were given a black number on a white square. Special features, such as projecting corbel stones, the 'squint' between the aisle and the chancel, the bell-cote and the aumbrey at the east end of the aisle were detailed separately. Items such as the flagstones in the porch and the remains of the stock that once held the bell were also sketched, measured and recorded.

With the roof timbers, a slightly different method was used to identify each part. Instead of painted letters and figures, numbers were punched into small brass disks, which were then nailed to the timbers in question. Where two timbers met, as in a mortise and tenon joint, the corresponding parts of the timbers were given matching numbers. As with the masonry features, details of trusses, purlins and wall plates from different parts of the church were sketched, annotated, measured and recorded. Hundreds of photographs were taken of the building and of the dismantling process.

Pieces of part-glazed medieval clay ridge tiles were also discovered, including one that had survived intact. Evidence for the original roof covering was found in the churchyard walls, where old stone roofing tiles had been re-used as walling material, having been stripped off and replaced with Caernarfon slate in 1901.

(Right) Numbering the stonework around the north door before recording and dismantling the building. (1985)

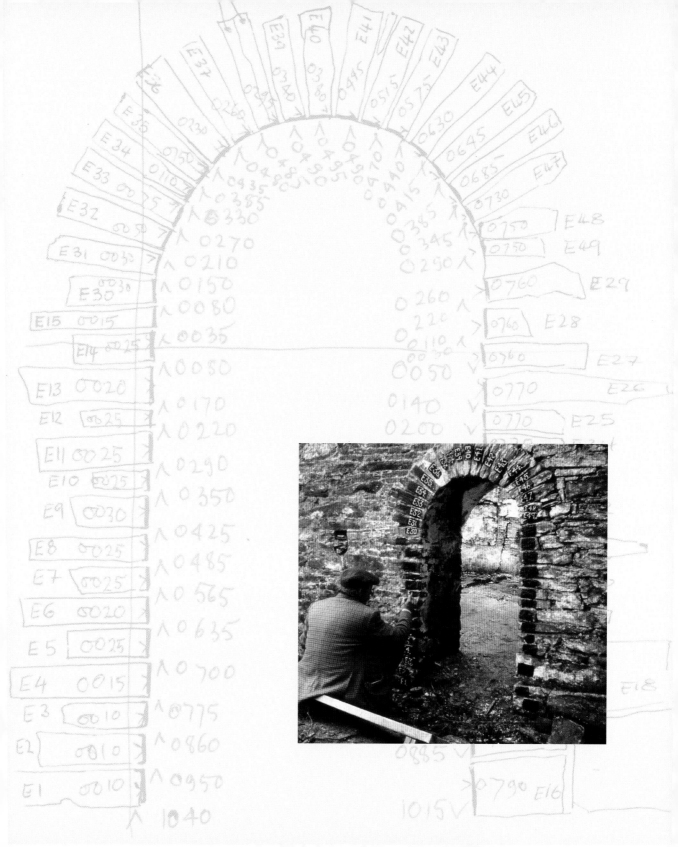

# Recovering the wall paintings

As noted, a survey of the church in the 1970s had identified traces of pigment under-neath flaked limewash, which signalled the possible survival of wall paintings. Conservation lecturers David Watkinson and David Leigh, together with conservators from the Museum, led a team of students from Cardiff University in a painstaking opera-tion to remove the multiple coats of limewash and reveal what lay beneath. Using scalpels and mechanical tools, the layers were scraped away, millimetre by millimetre; what was exposed was the most extensive set of medieval paintings yet discovered in Wales.

After the Reformation, church interiors were frequently limewashed for Easter. Over the centuries, this build-up of limewash had protected the underlying paint surfaces. Removing the layers required skill and innovation to ensure that no damage occurred to the paint and plaster beneath. For every area where limewash removal was simple and straightforward, other sections were challenging and difficult. This was often because of water from leaking roofs and penetrating damp dissolving the lime and car-rying it down the wall, where it was re-deposited as a hard crust as the water evapo-rated. In places, the underlying plaster had disappeared entirely due to the scouring effects of water, which produced voids that made the paint layer fragile.

The excitement of revealing the paintings was tempered by the difficult ethical deci-sions they posed. In places, perhaps only twenty-five years after the initial medieval paintings had been executed, over-painting had been carried out to modify an image or create a different one. Which paintings, therefore, should be revealed and preserved? We had to take into consideration the prevailing quality and condition of the paint lay-ers and the extent of their survival. For example, the removal of a well-preserved, slightly later painting to reveal fragments of an earlier painting offered important information on the painting sequence and its subject matter – but at the expense of losing the better-quality image. In such instances, the later image could be retained in the knowledge that the fragments of earlier painting survived underneath it. Conversely, a badly damaged over-painting might be removed to reveal a more com-plete earlier painting. Any over-painting that was removed was recorded. Since the church was to be disassembled, moved and rebuilt, it was now essential to lift the paintings to preserve them for posterity.

Following extensive tests, it was decided to use a version of the Italian *stacco* technique to protect the exposed paintings and lift them off the walls. The fragmenting and loose

paint surfaces were strengthened with an acrylic resin. Then layers of butter muslin and scrim were adhered over the top, using the same resin. On drying, the muslin/scrim facing shrank fast to the surface, forming a rigid support that followed the surface irregularities and three-dimensional character of the painting, and the underlying plaster. These could then be lifted off the wall with a variety of tools carefully inserted between the plaster and the underlying stone wall. As the removal proceeded, the facing on the painted/plaster surface held it together. The paintings were lowered backwards onto a board, ready for transport.

(Left) The image of St Catherine of Alexandria, dating from around 1400, as uncovered on the east wall of the aisle.

(Right) The same painting following removal from the church and conservation work carried out in 1986 and 2009.

Back at Cardiff University's laboratories, a rigid backing system was devised to support the paintings before removing the facings. The back of the lime plaster layer was levelled, missing areas were filled with more plaster and polyether foam applied to it. This formed a lightweight, reversible layer between the plaster and a backing of rigid fibreglass and polyester. The painting was then turned over and the facing was removed using an organic solvent to dissolve the adhesive. Missing areas of paint were painted-in to retain the shape and line of the original images and to aid interpretation. These areas are easily detected using ultraviolet light and are visible to the eye at close quarters. The end result, as well as creating an exciting visual experience, made the paintings easy to transport, store and display.

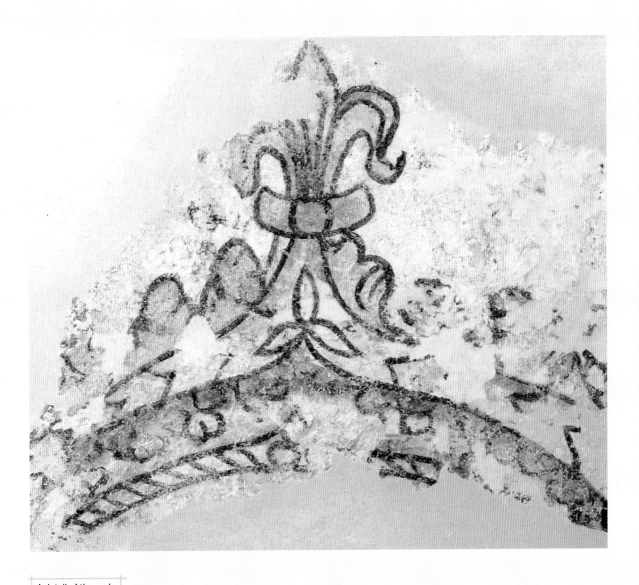

A detail of the early 15th-century 'canopy' above St Catherine. The artist's use of free-flowing lines and colour are well illustrated here.

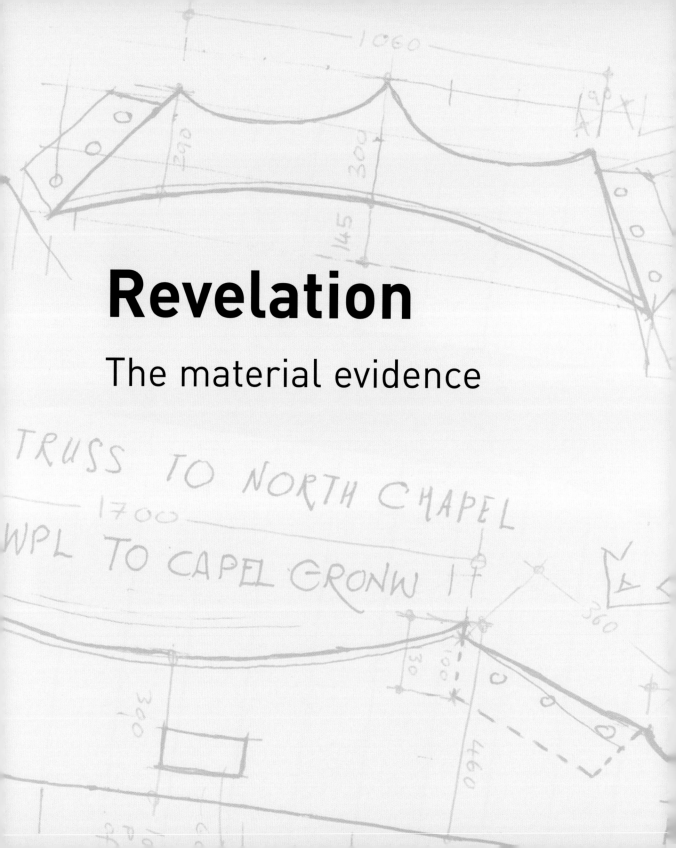

# Revelation

## The material evidence

The small, single-light window in the north wall of the nave, showing original and replacement stonework.

## Stone

A site for the church had already been identified within the Museum grounds. During the early 1980s a large stand of elm trees had been felled because of Dutch elm disease, and the resulting clearing provided an ideal setting, being flat if somewhat marshy – not unlike the church's original setting, in fact. The first task was to set out the foundations. Built of stone, like the walls, but wider and bonded with lime mortar, the foundations extended some one-and-a half metres below ground level.

The cross-datum lines (used to measure the church, as described on page 34) were set up around and through the building so that each of the numbered stones could be positioned. The masonry walls were then re-built, with each corner, doorway and window opening accurately located. Many of the external walls were 'battered', that is, they were thicker at the base and tapered gradually towards the top, creating a buttress effect, a feature common in medieval buildings. The wall at the west end was markedly battered for the first metre or so, and then continued upwards as a straight wall. Between these two parts, a line of projecting stones – a 'stringer' course – created a decorative horizontal band along the wall. Different parts of the building displayed different patterns of construction; for example, whereas most of the building was constructed of random rubble, the walls of the late fifteenth-century porch and the north wall of the nave featured double courses of large, round river pebbles between bands of thin flat sandstone.

Only one original medieval window had survived more or less intact, namely a small fourteenth-century two-light window in the south wall of the aisle. Even here, some of the masonry had suffered from decay and erosion, and parts of the heads had been chopped out when it was bricked up during the early twentieth century. To repair or replace these sections it was necessary first to identify the original stone used and, if possible, where it was quarried. Dr John Davies, Regional Geologist with the Countryside Council for Wales, confirmed that the stone was Cae-ras conglomerate (Lower Devonian brown-stone containing small quartz pebbles and other stones including Silurian sandstone and silt-stones with fossils), a seam of which ran quite close to the site of the church. This stone was also used for the eleventh-century font, which stood at the west end of the aisle. A long-abandoned section of Cil-yr-ychen quarry near Llandybie (about nine miles up-river from Llandeilo Tal-y-bont) yielded several large stones of identical composition and colour to the window stones. These were cut to shape and used to replace the missing sections of masonry. This same

New mullions and cinquefoil heads, carved using traditional methods, were incorporated in many of the windows where the original masonry no longer survived.

quarry may also have provided the limestone used for the lime in mortars, renders and limewash in the church.

All the other windows had been stripped of their original carved tracery and only one, at the east end of the aisle, still retained its carved surround. Many of these window openings had then been blocked up, presumably when new windows were inserted in the church in 1810. When these were uncovered during the recording process, it was found that many still had their original plastered sills and reveals, and that, consequently, many original paintings had survived.

Fortunately, three pieces of squared limestone blocks, which had been used to block up part of the chapel window, turned out to be sections of fifteenth-century carved window heads turned back-to-front so that the decorated side could not be seen. This discovery enabled the skilled banker masons to re-create the moulded cinquefoil heads that would have been found in the one- and two-light windows. When re-assembled, the pieces were found to fit the window openings exactly.

The most important window in the church, at the east end of the chancel, raised another question: should it have one, two or three openings, or 'lights'? It was known that the original window had been replaced in 1810 by a timber two-light lancet window. Later, this too was replaced when the east wall was rebuilt in 1927, this time by a tall, narrow, cast iron lancet-type window taken out of the 'new' St Teilo's when it was remodelled in 1905. A single-light window would have been unlikely when most of the other windows in the church had two lights. East windows tend to be larger than the others, often being divided into three lights, which made them ideal for painted glass depicting symbols of the Trinity. However, more than a third of medieval chancel windows recorded by the Museum in Glamorgan had just two lights. As there was no firm evidence for a larger window in the east wall, the decision was taken to create a two-light window, based on the others, but scaled-up slightly to suit its position above the high altar.

Internally, the most prominent features in the building are the five arches: two between the nave and the aisle, one between the chancel and the aisle, one between the chancel and the north chapel, and the largest – a tall elliptical arch – between the nave and chancel, namely the chancel arch. These had all been carefully surveyed, their widths and heights recorded and detailed measurements taken at 100-millimetre spacings. No two arches were alike, and neither were the corresponding sides of the same arch. This meant that great care had to be taken when setting out the outlines of the arches.

Most of them were simple half-round arches and built of rubble, the only slight hint at decoration being a plain chamfer to the square pillar-walls. There were no slender columns or ornately carved capitals; indeed, the simplicity of the arches, perhaps more than anything in the building, hinted at the relative poverty of the parish of Llandeilo Tal-y-bont during the Middle Ages.

The arches were reconstructed using the same basic principles as when they were first built. First, the pillars were built up in stone to the 'springers', or the points at which the arches started. Then, a timber formwork was made to the shape of each arch, and located so that the bottom of the arch corresponded with the

The north chapel doorway, as rebuilt, using numbered stonework.

(Top) Timber formwork was used to support the masonry of the nave arcade and the chancel arch.

(Bottom) Once the first layer of stonework had been built, the timberwork could be removed as the arches were then self-supporting.

springer points. Flat arch-stones were then built on top of, and at right angles to, the formwork, working from either side until they met at the centre, where the final stone, the key stone, served to lock them all in place. A similar technique was also used for building the arched door heads and relieving arches above some of the windows.

As the walls were built, they were limewashed. This was done to protect the surface of the masonry work, and in particular the lime mortar, to prevent it from drying out too quickly in summer (the white limewash serving to reflect a lot of the sun's rays), while providing some protection against frosts in winter. Once completed, the whole building was painted with six coats of limewash – a hot-lime mix was found to give the best results.

All the internal walls were covered in a lime-based plaster. This was applied in three coats: first, a fairly coarse base coat, followed by a second 'scratch' coat, which evened-out some of the irregularities in the masonry, and finally a thin skim coat, applied with a wooden float. The plastered walls were then painted with at least three coats of limewash, the final coat serving as a base for the wall paintings.

It is not known what sort of floor would have been found in the church during the early sixteenth century, but it may well have been made of beaten earth. However, the heavy visitor traffic at the Museum would soon destroy such a floor, and it was decided that a compromise would have to be found that would both withstand the wear and tear and be in keeping with the period. Sandstone flags appeared to offer the best solution, as these would have been available locally to medieval builders. Luckily, the Museum was offered a large quantity of suitable flagstones from a building that had been demolished just a few miles from the site of the church.

The roofs were originally covered with stone roofing tiles, almost certainly obtained from one of the many nearby quarries, where suitable, easily splittable stone came near to the surface. These tiles were laid in diminishing courses, that is, the longest slabs were laid nearest the bottom of the roof, the eaves, and then gradually these diminished in length further up the roof. Towards the top

One of the arcade arches, viewed through the south doorway.

The north chapel roof showing stone tiles laid in diminishing courses, with glazed clay tiles along the ridge.

of each tile, in the centre, a small hole was drilled. A small, slightly tapered oak peg was pushed into this hole so that it projected through the other side, and, being wedge-shaped, was held in place. This peg enabled the tile to be 'hung' on one of the many rows of cleft chestnut battens that were nailed onto the roof rafters. The larger stone tiles often had two such pegs to help hold their weight. It is estimated that some 8,000 stone tiles were needed to cover St Teilo's church.

At the apex of the roof, ridge tiles were required to make the roof water-tight. The fortunate discovery of a complete medieval ridge tile, and several broken fragments, enabled the Museum to commission accurate replicas, which were fixed onto the tops of the roofs with lime mortar.

### A happy coincidence

In 2006, the opportunity arose to learn more about how lime was produced in the Middle Ages. Coinciding with a meeting of the Building Limes Forum at St Fagans, a request came to construct a replica of a thirteenth-century lime kiln, based on substantial remains that had been found at Cilgerran Castle in Pembrokeshire. The kiln was constructed and successfully fired using different limestones and different types of coal, and quicklime was produced which was then used to make mortar and limewash.

Each stone tile was held in place by an oak peg which, enabled it to be hung on one of the cleft chestnut battens.

Five pairs of new oak trusses were made for the chancel roof to replace timbers inserted in the late 18th century.

Ray Smith, Head Carpenter with the Museum's Historic Buildings Unit, examining some of the roof trusses in the south aisle.

## Wood

### The Roof

The roof structure offered quite a challenge to the Museum's carpenters. Many of the timbers had suffered from the effects of exposure to weather and rain, not to mention insect attack. Several had already been repaired at least once in the past and some had been re-used in different locations. It was known, for instance, that the timbers in the chancel were not original – a point confirmed by the date 1780 carved onto one of the collars.

The remaining trusses and purlins in the nave, aisle, porch and north chapel were less easily dated. While they were all more or less similar in design – the space between the collar and trusses being formed as a distinctive cusped trefoil – those in the north chapel had a much more medieval 'feel' than those in the nave. It was therefore decided to try to date the timbers using dendrochronology – a technique where the pattern of tree-ring spacing is matched to a known series of dateable tree rings by computer. The outermost, sapwood layer would indicate the date when the tree was felled, sometimes to within a month or two. As structural timbers were usually used 'green', that is, freshly cut, it is often possible to calculate the date at which the timber was used.

Three trusses remained in the north chapel, but it was clear that there was once a fourth, which had been removed at some stage. Replicating the missing truss gave the carpenters an opportunity to study at first hand the techniques their medieval counterparts would have used to cut, carve and finish a medieval roof. All of this work was done by hand, from cutting the mortises and tenons and shaping the cusps using chisels, mallets and saws, to running the decorative mouldings along the lower edges of the trusses with moulding planes, chisels and scrapers, and finally creating a smooth finish with an adze. When it came to the roof timbers in the south aisle and porch it was found that, even though many of the mortise and tenon joints had failed, it would still be possible to re-use many of the original timbers by carefully cutting out the damaged sections and jointing or 'scarfing-in' new pieces. Loading tests were carried out at the University of Glamorgan to confirm that the old timbers could still support the weight of the heavy stone-tiled roof.

The trusses in the nave turned out to be seventeenth-century replacements and made of much poorer quality oak, and with less sharply defined cusping and mouldings than those in the north chapel. Most were also in very poor condition, with extensive areas of rot and breaks at critical points such as the ridge and collar joints. It was therefore

decided to re-create the whole of the nave and chancel roofs, using the original trusses in the north chapel as patterns, scaled-up and adjusted to suit the respective widths. For technical reasons it was not possible to date the other timbers accurately, but comparison with other buildings in the locality suggested that they were earlier, and probably medieval.

The distinctive cusped trefoils formed between the trusses and collars.

The newly built
roof of the chancel,
viewed towards
the chancel arch
and nave.

## The Rood Screen

The design of a medieval church was based on the idea that the building became progressively more holy, and therefore less accessible, the further east you moved. The altar in the chancel, or sanctuary, represented the most holy place, so between the nave and the chancel there was always a symbolic barrier, which could normally be crossed only by the clergy. In parish churches this would be a screen of wood, or occasionally of stone.

Typically the screen would have had a central doorway and open panels to either side, through which the congregation could see the priest celebrating Mass at the high altar. Above the screen there

would be a canopy supporting a platform with panelling to front and back. The upper beam of the panelling supported carvings of the crucified Christ flanked by the Virgin Mary and St John, known as the 'rood'. These figures would have been the focus for much of the devotion and as such were a target at the Reformation. Most were destroyed, although a few were hidden – one such may be the figure from Kemeys Inferior in Monmouthshire. At the counter-Reformation under Mary Tudor some were put back, but in other cases they were replaced by a painted Crucifixion scene. This was probably the case at St Teilo's church, where there were traces of a Crucifixion painted on the apex of the chancel arch.

There would also have been 'parclose' screens separating the north and south chapels from the chancel, and possibly a screen across the aisle. These would have been similar to the rood screen in design, but usually with doors and without lofts.

The hand-carved and brightly decorated rood screen, viewed from the nave. Gold leaf was used to highlight many of the finer lines and details.

Very few screens remain in south Wales; most of those that survived the Reformation or the systematic destruction following the Civil War fell victim to the neglect of the eighteenth century and the enthusiasm of Victorian restorers. However, although there was nothing left of the screen at St Teilo's church, clear evidence remained. On either side of the chancel arch were stone corbels, which would have supported the beam at the back of the loft. Higher up, and to one side of the chancel arch, there was a doorway that would have opened onto the loft, and behind it a sloping chase that must have held a wooden ladder.

Comparison with similar churches in south Wales, the Marches and south-west England suggest that the screen would have been fitted within the chancel arch while the loft spanned the full width of the nave, and so this was the pattern chosen for the reconstruction. The central doorway is flanked by open cusped lancets above a panelled dado, based on examples from the Vale of Glamorgan. There are no doors, as the surviving screens have no evidence for hinges or locks. The ribbed soffit and blind arcading on the front, in twelve compartments, are based on examples in the Marches. The beams supporting the loft and the highly decorated mouldings and vine-scrolls are also based on original examples. Since some examples include scenes from the life of the saint to which the church is dedicated, notably St Melangell at Pennant Melangell, it was decided to recreate a sequence of episodes from the life of St Teilo. These are reduced to a simple 'strip-cartoon' style, which could have been followed by people of the time who knew the legends of the saint. The carvings have been modelled on contemporary carvings, such as a frieze on a bedstead from Derwydd in Carmarthenshire.

Like the rest of the church, the rood screen would have been painted. Traces of colour in screens such as those at Newtown and Llangattock Lingoed confirm that mouldings were picked out with colour and gilding, and sometimes with patterns such as chevrons or barber pole-style stripes. References in poetry describe loft fronts painted with the Apostles; surviving paintings from south-west England depict them either carrying their identifying symbols – which usually indicate their martyrdom – or carrying scrolls with clauses from the Apostles' Creed. There were well-known conventions for depicting the apostles – Peter, for instance was always shown with a square beard, John as a young man and Paul as bald with a pointed beard – and this, combined with

The friezes, panels and mouldings were carved by the Museum's Head Carpenter, Ray Smith.

Artist Fleur Kelly, painting one of the Apostles on the front of the rood loft.

their symbols, would have made them instantly recognisable to the congregation of the time (see also page 96).

On the end of the reconstructed screen are symbols of the Passion. There is also the craftsman's monogram and the date of completion, a feature which is sometimes found concealed in the carving of original screens. The parclose screens, which are not quite as elaborate as the rood screen, are based on features recorded at Gwernesney and elsewhere.

The medieval wooden statues from Kemeys Inferior and Mochdre provided models for the carved figures on top of the loft, and also show that these statues were brightly painted, like all the other statues in the church. As with the paintings, the carvings stress the humanity of Jesus in his sufferings, and the pain endured by those standing by. The statues are a visual parallel to the words and the symbolic action repeated at every celebration of the Mass, and a constant reminder to worshippers that their salvation was achieved at unimaginable cost.

## Glass

The medieval stained glass that survives so impressively in many of Britain's great cathedrals and parish churches shows how important glazed windows were to Christian worshippers in the Middle Ages. An important question for the St Teilo's team was whether the medieval congregations of this rather small and remote Welsh church also had decorative glass windows to reinforce their spiritual learning.

No fragments of medieval window glass have yet been found on the original site of St Teilo's, and no documentary evidence for windows has come to light. Luckily however, the remains of two medieval windows found during the dismantling of the church do suggest that it probably was glazed. The two-light, stone-mullioned window of the late fourteenth or early fifteenth century, discovered beneath lime wash and render at the east end of the aisle, has a rebated arch detail to allow some kind of window to be fitted on its inner face. The other window, the top part of a two-light, cinquefoil cusped window found in the east wall of the chapel, was probably part of an extensive refurbishment of the church in the late fifteenth century. The stonework has a glazing groove cut into it as well as rebates for *ferramenta* (iron bars to which the window leadwork was tied), the best evidence that this and all the other significant windows were glazed. It is reasonable to assume that, except for the earlier window, the same window pattern was used throughout the church at this time.

The challenge was to find evidence for what kind of windows these might have been. Wales is home to some very fine medieval stained glass windows, many of them dated to about 1485-1515, the right period for comparison with St Teilo's. Unfortunately, these are nearly all in north Wales and in much grander churches like Llanrhaeadr, Llandyrnog or Gresford. North-Walian windows can suggest appropriate subjects and compositions, or suitable leaf and flower designs for painted quarries (the small glass panels), but are not directly relevant to St Teilo's.

Evidence for medieval stained glass in south Wales is extremely scarce and fragmentary. The fact that so little survives suggests that glazed windows, and especially elaborate expensive ones, were probably always rare. In Monmouthshire scattered fragments of medieval pictorial windows remain at a number of churches, such as St Cadoc's in Llangattock Lingoed. Here the windows were apparently smashed in the middle of the seventeenth century and replaced with low-quality plain quarries of greenish glass, but elements survive of earlier windows of various dates. These include

(Following pages) Symbols of the Passion have been painted onto some of the hand-made glass quarries of the chancel window by students from the Welsh School of Architectural Glass, Swansea Metropolitan University.

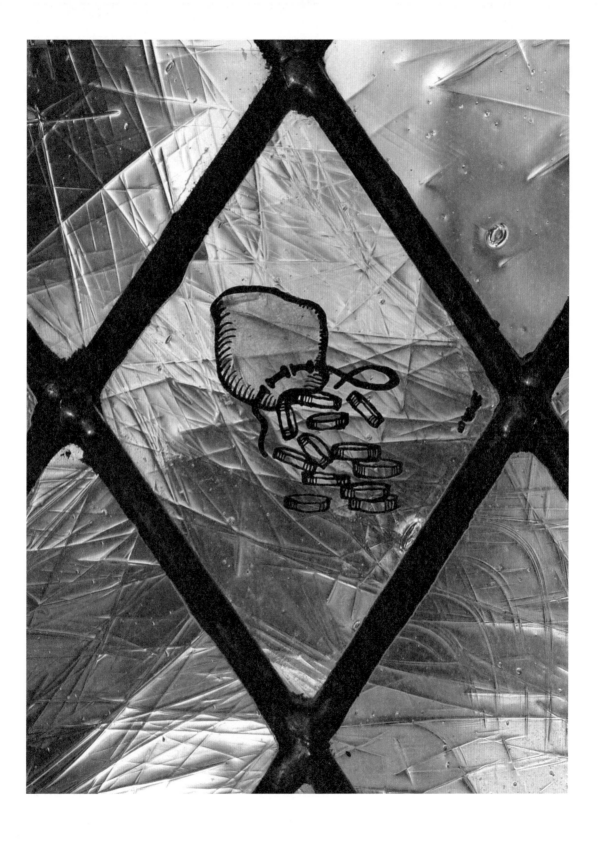

a painted grisaille Tree of Life window of the thirteenth century, a window with a canopy of the fourteenth century and another of the late fifteenth or early sixteenth century featuring part of a chequered floor. At least some of the traceries were in plain white glass.

Elsewhere in Monmouthshire, late fifteenth-century fragments fill the west window of the south aisle at St Tewdric's in Mathern, including armorial panels associated with John Marshall, Bishop of Llandaff (1478-96). St Bridget's in Skenfrith has numerous fourteenth- to sixteenth-century quarries, borders and a repeated crown motif in the east window of the chancel. The north chancel window at St Mary the Virgin in Llanfair Cilgedin also contains medieval fragments. The most intact survival is a panel featuring St George in the house of Great Cil-Llwch in Llantilio Crossenny, perhaps removed from the nearby church – also called St Teilo's.

Excavated evidence also supports the existence of certain window types that might have adorned St Teilo's. Plain diaper glass has been excavated at Llanthony Abbey in Monmouthshire. In Cardiff, fragments from the Blackfriars and Greyfriars sites provide examples of painted grisaille glass as well as geometric, architectural and leaf border patterns. Further west, excavations at Carmarthen Greyfriars have revealed not only numerous glass fragments with ivy-leaf decoration, but also remains of two window panels with similar simple geometric borders, both incorporating some painted decoration and red and blue coloured glass. Most interestingly, one of these panels features a coat of arms that is probably that of Walter Bluet, Deputy Justiciar at Carmarthen Castle in 1380, suggesting a late fourteenth-century date.

Evidence from the wealthy Cistercian Abbey at Neath, within whose possessions Llandeilo Tal-y-bont lay, also lends weight to the case for glazed windows at St Teilo's. In 1504 the abbey received a bequest towards glazing its west window. The poet Lewis Morgannwg visited in about 1520, describing it as 'a palace comparable to the temple of Solomon' and noting that there were coats of arms in the glazed windows. It is possible that St Teilo's had at least one armorial window commemorating a local donor, perhaps in what came to be know as the Gronow Chapel. The Gronow coat of arms has not yet been identified, but fourteenth-century armorial tiles from Neath Abbey could provide a plausible alternative such as John de Norris, a benefactor of the Abbey.

Initially, the church has been glazed with hand-blown plain white quarry windows, which enabled work to begin on the wall paintings and allowed time for appropriate windows to be designed, commissioned, made and installed. For the future, a scheme

has been proposed that reflects the modest character of the church, its various building phases and, for a church that may have been on one of the pilgrimage routes to St David's, the possibility of periodic benefactions. The two-light windows will work best with paired subjects. The Gronow Chapel could have a donor figure and a coat of arms in a style of about 1400. The chancel east window, in a late fifteenth-century style, could feature paired saints like David and Teilo, or contrasting Old and New Testament subjects, or a Crucifixion and Resurrection. Other windows in the church could have plain diamond quarries or possibly quarries with painted flower or leaf motifs. The rood loft light could be made of horn and the square-headed single light in the Gronow Chapel gable could be left unglazed or covered with waxed linen.

Surviving evidence within the church itself could contribute to the design of the windows. For example, the painted border patterns and an as yet unidentified coat of arms could be echoed in the windows. It will be most important, though, to study surviving windows in areas of Britain of comparable character to south-west Wales. Interesting glass can be found in some of the smaller and more remote churches of north Wales, such as the rather naïve early-sixteenth-century St Christopher at Dolwyddelan in Snowdonia. Most useful, however, are Cornwall, with its comparable devotion to local saints, north Devon and to some extent Gloucestershire, where a number of relatively modest churches feature figures of saints and donors, coats of arms and patterned borders and quarries. St David's Priory in Swansea has a fifteenth-century Resurrection window that is thought to have come from Devon.

Given that any decorative windows installed in St Teilo's will be largely speculative, it has been important to be cautious, and to take time to develop as plausible and authentic a scheme as possible. Eventually, though, it is hoped that visitors to the reconstructed church will, in the words of the twelfth-century German monk Theophilus in his treatise on stained glass, be able to enjoy 'the profusion of light from the windows ... the inestimable beauty of the glass and the infinitely rich and various workmanship.'

## Ceramics

Ceramic tiles for roof ridges were made in England and Wales from the late thirteenth century, and were in common use into the early sixteenth century. Specialist potter John Hudson re-created ridge tiles for St Teilo's based on a surviving late medieval example found at the church. Like the original ridge tiles, the replicas have crests that have been trimmed by a blade. Combed wavy lines or grooves, as was common, decorate the ridge tile; stabbing in the sides of the crests – in this case, made by the tiler's fingers – made shallow vertical grooves and a tool was used to make triangular impressions. In the thirteenth/fourteenth-century the Cardiff/Barry area was dominated by products of the Vale-ware industry, and its pottery vessels were traded along the coast as far as Gower, Carmarthen and Monmouthshire. That Vale-ware ridge tiles were made near Cardiff has been confirmed by the discovery in 2001 of wasters (imperfect, discarded pieces) outside the Bishop's Castle at Llandaff, which was started by Bishop William de Braose (1266-87). However, the design of the surviving Llandeilo Tal-y-bont ridge tile resembles ridge tiles found in south-west Wales, which suggests a more local source for St Teilo's.

Floors paved in earthenware tiles began to appear in Britain in the eleventh century, though initial use was restricted to large abbeys. While they became hugely fashionable among the English elite during the thirteenth century and remained in use until the sixteenth century and beyond, they were too expensive ever to come into general use. Beaten earth and stone slabs provided floor coverings for most buildings, including church naves. Nevertheless, high altars and side altars in parish churches might have had areas of tiling, either directly at floor level or on a raised step (the *predella* or footpace). Floor tiles have been recorded at a number of parish churches in

Surviving medieval glazed ridge tiles, like this one found near the original church, were used as patterns for making the replicas.

Replica floor tiles, made by John Hudson from Mirfield, West Yorkshire, were based on green and yellow medieval glazed tiles found in several south Wales churches.

south Wales, such as St John the Baptist in Cardiff, Carew-Cheriton in Cosheston, St Mary's in Newtown, St John's in Slebech and St Mary's in Tenby. Some are inlaid tiles, while others are plain.

While no floor tile fragments were found at St Teilo's church, some late fifteenth- or sixteenth-century enrichment of the floor around the altars would be in accordance with the considerable sum laid out to decorate the walls. During this period distinctive floor tiles with a light-coloured fabric and bright yellow and green glazes were imported from France, probably somewhere in the Seine Valley, in order to meet the demand of re-flooring monastic houses. There are records of consignments being exported via Rouen and Le Havre between about 1490 and 1530. They have been found in buildings of varying scale, often with monastic connections of some sort. In view of the association between Neath Abbey and St Teilo's church, John Hudson was commissioned to replicate the glazed French imports found at Neath Abbey, based on fragments from the Museum's collections. The result is a striking green and gold chequered pattern.

# The bell

By the early eighteenth century, the original bell in St Teilo's church had been replaced by a new bell cast by William Evans's foundry in Chepstow and dated 1728. It was installed in the new bell-cote when the west gable wall of the nave was rebuilt in 1736; this was recorded by a stone plaque set into the wall, bearing the letters 'W I:E' and the date. Unfortunately, this bell disappeared during the 1970s, shortly after the church stopped being used for the monthly summer annual services. The Museum therefore decided to commission a new bell, but cast to a medieval design that would be appropriate to the refurbished building. After much searching, a suitable fifteenth-century bell was found in St Illtyd's Church in Llantwit Major. Although no longer in use and quite badly cracked, it displayed all the features that typified medieval church bells and was therefore chosen as a pattern for the new bell.

The bell-foundry selected to cast it, in 2006, was Taylor, Eayre & Smith, in Loughborough, who are probably best known for casting the largest bell in Britain, namely 'Great Paul' in St Paul's Cathedral, in 1881. Though of more modest proportions, the bell for St Teilo's church has also been cast using centuries-old techniques and, like many medieval bells, it has a prayer in Latin around the crown, reading *SANCTE TELIAVE ORA PRO NOBIS*, which translates as 'St Teilo, pray for us'.

(Left) Preparing the mould for casting the bell at Taylor, Eayre and Smith's foundry in Loughborough. (2006)

(Right) The new bell, made to a medieval design, installed in the bell-cote.

## Paint

From the beginning of Christianity as a persecuted sect in the Roman Empire, Christians have painted the walls of their buildings. These paintings were intended as a spiritual tool for teaching and to aid prayer and devotion. In Britain, paintings survive from the tenth/eleventh century onwards, and they show that, as in other aspects of organized religion, churches in Wales used the same range of designs and images as the whole of western Christendom.

A medieval church was quite unlike its modern counterpart. Far from a quiet haven of white plaster, it was peopled by saints and angels, with a riot of colour, designed to help a largely illiterate congregation to understand and participate in the mystery of salvation played out weekly in the service of the Mass. Paintings were a way of teaching people what they should believe and how they should live their Christian lives. Scenes from the Bible outlined the story of salvation 'from the time of our first disobedience' by Adam and Eve to the apocalyptic vision of the Last Judgement. The Lives of the Saints showed how others had lived and died for their faith. Finally, symbolic pictures with strongly moral messages would hammer home the practical outworkings of theology and ethical teachings. While preachers – both resident clergy and travelling friars – expounded many of these teachings, the church building itself contained daily reminders in a form that everyone could understand.

For various reasons, there are relatively few surviving medieval wall paintings in Welsh churches. However, there are examples of each of the major groups of subjects that are found throughout Britain.

Firstly, there were figures and scenes from the Bible, but focusing on the life, death, resurrection and Second Coming of Jesus Christ. The fundamental teaching of the church, then as now, was the message of salvation – that Jesus came to earth to save sinners, and that he was the Messiah or Christ foretold through the Old Testament and revealed to mankind in the New Testament. So it is not surprising that the majority of paintings concentrated on the story of Christ. Only two subjects from the Old Testament are known from Wales: a possible King David at St Stephen's in Llanstephan, and Adam and Eve at St Ellyw's in Llanelieu.

By far the most important paintings were those relating to the story of Jesus, from his birth – there is an Adoration of the Magi on the chancel ceiling at St Elian's in

(Right) Part of the Deposition, showing Christ being lowered from the Cross. The painting, executed using natural pigments, is based on an early 16th-century woodcut.

St Christopher,
viewed in his
usual position
opposite the
south doorway.

Llanelian-yn-Rhos – to his Passion and death – as at St Wyddyn's in Llanwddyn, regrettably destroyed, and crucifixions at St David's Cathedral and St Mary's in Tenby.

Almost every church would contain a painting of the final event in the story of salvation, namely the Last Judgement. The most common location would have been above the chancel arch, at the liturgical division between the area for the people and the area for the clergy, symbolic of the division between earth and heaven. The only surviving example from Wales, at St Giles in Wrexham, shows the risen Christ seated on a rainbow, flanked by saints and angels carrying the emblems of the Passion. At his feet the dead are emerging from their graves, and on either side are the blessed going into the heavenly city and the damned disappearing into the jaws of hell. A simplified version remains on rood screen panels from Llanelian-yn-Rhos; this includes St Michael weighing souls, which is also depicted at St Cybi's in Llangybi.

Secondly, there were scenes from the lives of the Saints, often legendary in character. Sometimes these were isolated depictions like the two Marys at Llantwit Major, or sometimes a scene such as St George and the dragon at Llancarfan. A pair of scenes at Colwinston depicts two events from the life of St Nicholas, and there might have been a large-scale cycle of the life of St Winifred at Holywell.

One saint above all, however, was to be found in almost every church, and in a fairly constant location: that was St Christopher. According to late medieval superstition, because of his name, 'the Christ-bearer', to look on the image of St Christopher could help you achieve a 'good' death, in other words one with the opportunity to prepare, be reconciled with God, and receive the sacraments of the Church. His picture was therefore placed opposite the main doorway, so that the faithful could simply look in without even having to enter the building. Two elaborate examples of this survive, at Llantwit Major and Llanynys. In each, St Christopher, wielding a huge staff and carrying the Christ-child on his shoulder, wades across a fish-infested river; on the bank stands a diminutive hermit with a lamp in front of his cell.

Thirdly, there were other figures and scenes with moralistic content, often derived from medieval legends. The legend of the Three Living and the Three Dead (in which three skeletons confront a hunting party, with the message 'what I am, you will be'), may have been painted at Llancarfan. A more cheerful scene, the Seven Acts of Mercy as described in Matthew 25, was discovered remarkably preserved at Ruabon, where a series of vignettes shows merciful donors, each propelled by an angel, helping the unfortunate – the hungry, the thirsty, the naked and so on. The contrasting Seven Deadly Sins remain at Llangar as a series of emblematic animals with riders: the boar (gluttony), lion (pride) and stag (lechery) can be identified.

More frequent is the picture known as the Sunday Christ, in which the wounded Christ is surrounded by the tools of everyday life. The message is that Christ still suffers as a result of the sins committed in everyday life, in particular that of working on the Sabbath. A complete example survives at Llangybi.

By the end of the Middle Ages there was increasing theological argument about paintings, centred on the perceived risk that paintings as well as statues might become objects of worship in their own right. Following the Reformation a series of official instructions – the latest after the Civil War – required the removal of paintings from churches, and their replacement by texts from the Bible or the Prayer Book. This changed the entire face of church decoration; churches were whitewashed, and in their place came painted texts, some in English, some in Welsh, depending on the date and the dominant language of the parish. After the Restoration in 1660 the Royal Arms was also regularly displayed, a good example of which was at Llangar.

Most of these were also removed during Victorian restorations. However, much still survives under limewash, and is being revealed during sympathetic repairs, like the recent discoveries at Newton Nottage and Llancarfan.

### The wall paintings at St Teilo's

The church at St Teilo's had wall paintings from at least seven separate dates. The earliest that we know of included an elegant painting of St Catherine, dated to the early fifteenth century on the basis of her costume. She had a high forehead, long fair hair, a halo and coronet; she stood in front of a spiked wheel and carried a sword in her right hand, the symbols of her martyrdom. Over this layer was painted the early sixteenth-century sequence that has been reproduced in the rebuilt church, telling the story of the Passion along with paintings of saints and angels.

At the Reformation, all the visible paintings were covered with limewash. Traces of a Crucifixion on the chancel arch might date from the reign of Queen Mary, replacing the carved rood figures destroyed in the time of Edward VI. After the Reformation, church walls were still decorated, but with texts rather than pictures. Fragments of two

The arrest of Christ in the Garden of Gethsemane, painted on the north wall of the nave; based on an early 16th-century woodcut.

Paternosters in Welsh survived from the later sixteenth century. On the north wall of the chancel was an inscription inside an arched frame with orange 'jewelling'. The style of the black-letter script suggests a pre-Civil War date. The final major repainting of the church took place in 1715, when almost every wall of the church was repainted in the most up-to-date style. An inscription in fine calligraphic Roman lettering recorded the date of the repainting and the names of the church-wardens. On the north wall of the nave was a massive Royal Arms, and the remains of an eighteenth-century Lord's Prayer in English inside an imitation picture-frame with delicate red 'carving'. On the opposite side of the church, on the east end of the south wall of the aisle, were the Ten Commandments in two large arched panels. On the north side of the chancel arch was a fragmentary inscription from Isaiah 52:7, on top of which were the remains of a late-eighteenth-century inscription.

The paintings that were of particular interest, however, were those painted between about 1490 and 1530. The Passion sequence is the most detailed surviving in Wales. It is typical of the late medieval focus on the brutal reality of Christ's sufferings. Blood streams from his wounds and his eyes are anguished and sorrowful. However, in other ways this sequence of paintings is quite unique. The story was told not in chronological order, but as a series of meditations on the event and the artefacts involved – the 'Instruments of the Passion'. Prayers and meditations focusing on the Instruments were an important part of late medieval devotion, but while they were often carved or painted on shields on church roofs, rood screens and tombs, it is unusual to find them used in wall paintings.

Above the lintel of the window in the middle of the north aisle was the Mocking of Christ at his trial. In the centre, full face, was the figure of Christ, with a halo and large, almost hypnotic eyes. It is difficult now to see the crown of thorns but blood drips down his forehead and face. To right and left are two men in profile, deliberately caricatured with bulbous noses and exaggerated expressions of hatred. They are spitting, and drops of spittle fall from Christ's face. The left-hand figure is wearing a hat with a flat crown and a turned-up brim with elaborate cut-outs, and this suggests a date in the late fifteenth century at the earliest.

On the east splay of the same window there was an angel, carrying a shield bearing the Three Nails, one of the traditional Instruments of the Passion. The figure looks into the window, as if to suggest that more of the story was to be found in painted glass. Opposite this, on the south wall of the nave, was the picture known as the Image of Pity. This was a very popular devotional image of the early sixteenth century, and showed Christ, clothed only in a loin-cloth and showing the wounds of the Crucifixion, seated

The Mocking of Christ is one of the most graphic and sobering images uncovered in the church. The original painting, now on display in National Museum Cardiff, was painted around 1500.

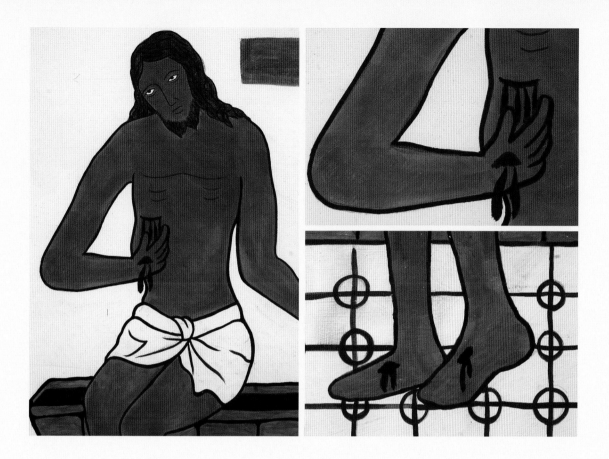

on a stone-built tomb. Medieval woodcuts often showed this figure surrounded by the Instruments of the Passion. To the west of this picture on the south wall of the nave was a more or less life-size figure, dressed in a striped doublet and close-fitting striped breeches, possibly part of a Deposition.

The final identifiable element in the series was on the east wall of the aisle, a painting of Christ before the crucifixion, sometimes known as 'Christ's last rest', inside a painted architectural 'niche'. Below an angular scroll with the words *Ecce homo* Christ was seated, wearing the Crown of Thorns. He had a fleur-de-lys halo, and there were streaks of blood on his face. His wrists, knees and ankles were bound with rope, and near his feet was a large skull, a visual reminder that the crucifixion took place at Golgotha, 'the place of the skull'. In medieval tradition the skull was believed to be that of Adam, so this picture encapsulates the whole story of human sin and redemption: 'for as in Adam all die, so in Christ all will be made alive' (1 Cor.15:22). To the left of the painting stood a ladder and a spear, two more of the Instruments of the Passion.

Christ displaying His wounds; a popular subject and focus of meditation and prayer in the late Middle Ages.

Slightly to the east of the window in the north wall containing the Passion Angel was another painting, more than half of which was destroyed by the insertion of a tall window in 1810. This depicted a haloed figure seated on a throne with the right hand raised in blessing. When this was first discovered, it was thought to represent Christ in glory, as described in the Book of the Revelation of St John. However, an inscription below the panel probably read *Sancta Trinitas*... ('Holy Trinity'). It is therefore likely that the picture actually showed the Trinity – God the Father on his throne, carrying the crucified Son and with the Holy Spirit shown as a dove.

The other paintings from this late medieval sequence were saints and angels, architectural decoration and linking borders. On the central pier of the arcade, in his traditional location immediately opposite the main doorway, was St Christopher. All that remained of the central figures were the haloed head of a child and, slightly lower down, a second, cruciform halo, and parts of the saint's cloak, body and right hand. To the left was an elaborate church, and in front was a robed figure carrying a rosary – presumably the hermit who charged Christopher with the task of carrying travellers across the river.

On the north side of the chancel arch were the badly damaged remains of the figure of an archbishop, wearing a mitre, chasuble and maniple, and carrying a cross-ended staff over his left shoulder. It probably represented St Thomas of Canterbury, one of the most popular saints in late medieval Britain. It is impossible to say whether the damage was accidental, or deliberate iconoclasm following Henry VIII's attack on the cult of St Thomas in 1538.

Several of the window splays had paintings of saints or angels, and it seems likely that in each window embrasure a saint on the left faced an angel on the right. On the east splay of the south-east window of the aisle was a figure with a wide-brimmed hat, a striped jacket with wide sleeves, short striped breeches, red hose and black shoes. Across his body was a narrow diagonal belt. He held a staff with an elaborate ferrule, and a pilgrim's scrip with long tassels. Originally identified as St James the Great, patron saint of pilgrims, this is more likely to be St Roche, patron of the plague-stricken, who is always depicted wearing contemporary costume. Facing him was an angel, standing full face with the right hand raised in front of the chest and the left hand pointing slightly downwards.

St Margaret and the dragon, with Passion angel opposite, painted on either side of a window in the south aisle.

Further along the south wall of the aisle was a blocked window, above which was the outline of a symmetrical decorated ogee arch with a fleur-de-lys finial. The outlines of shields could be seen above the two spandrels. On the eastern splay was the poorly preserved figure of a female saint, wearing a high hat or headdress, full-length robe with hanging sleeves and possibly a mantle faced with ermine, and holding a diagonal staff. She might represent St Margaret of Antioch, who is generally shown carrying a book and spearing a dragon beneath her feet, and often found depicted alongside St Catherine. On the west splay was the badly damaged outline of an angel, possibly carrying a shield. The figure, with long, flowing hair and almond-shaped eyes, stood full face but looking into the window.

On the south splay of the east window were the remains of what might have been another angel, wearing a long robe. Traces of an inscription remained at the top of the splay, and across the picture was an angular scroll with fragments of another inscription. Below the window sill was a damaged rectangular panel containing an inscription arranged around the outline of a cross, probably the reredos (or backing) for an altar.

Two walls in the Gronow Chapel retained significant paintings. On the north wall there were two unidentified figures separated and surrounded by a red and black geometric border. The left-hand figure, nearly life-size, was a priest or bishop in a short red cape and full-length white robe (perhaps an alb), possibly carrying a diagonal staff. The right-hand figure was poorly preserved, but areas of drapery could be seen. North of the partly blocked east window was another panel with figure-designs in red and black line. The figure was badly damaged, but the drapery suggested a seated female. It has been suggested that this might be a Virgin and Child, and that the standing figures were two of the Magi. The north side of a church was traditionally the women's side, and north chapels were often dedicated to the Virgin Mary. On one of the reveals of the window was the face of an unidentified female saint, wearing a head-dress or hood with a patterned brow-band typical of the early 1500s.

Not all the paintings in the church were directly associated with religious belief. Immediately above the Image of Pity was a shield with the Royal Arms surrounded by a Garter. This might indicate that the patron who sponsored the repainting of the church was closely associated with the Tudors: possibly the local marcher lord, Charles Somerset, 1st Earl of Worcester, or Sir Rhys ap Thomas of Dinefwr, both of whom were Knights of the Garter. An inscription below the Mocking of Christ might have been a version of *Heb Dduw Heb Ddim* ('Without God, Without Anything'), the motto of the Stradling family, to whom Sir Rhys ap Thomas's wife was related.

A final unusual feature in the St Teilo's wall paintings is the presence of a considerable amount of writing. Considering that most medieval worshippers could not read, the decoration of medieval churches often contained a surprising amount of text. Saints and scenes from the Bible in stained glass windows were identified by short scrolls, the Apostles in windows or on screens were often depicted with their clauses of the Apostles' Creed and depictions of the Annunciation frequently included the opening words of the *Ave Maria*. Writing in wall paintings, however, was unusual, and the St Teilo's wall paintings are virtually unique in having – admittedly short – inscriptions on scrolls below or integrated into the paintings.

The view towards the west door of the nave, showing scenes from the Passion of Christ on the walls and St Michael weighing souls above the doorway.

The texts are even more difficult to decipher and reconstruct than the paintings. In a panel to the left of the Image of Pity was a fragmentary black-letter inscription reading '*A dent ... Jhu mer...*' which seems to be a prayer, possibly a short section from a litany: '*A dentibus mortis* [from the jaws of death], *Jesu mercy*'. Above the shoulder of the Image of Pity might be a little more of the same litany: all that remained were the letters '*Jsu m...*' (possibly 'Jesu mercy' again, or its Latin equivalent '*Jesu miserere*'). At the west end of the north wall of the nave were the letters '*...homo da...*' which might be part of another prayer – *Jesu Christe, deus et homo, da nobis...* (Jesus Christ, God and Man, give us... ). As with certain key parts of the Latin mass, the priest would have taught his congregation what the words in these inscriptions were, and they would have guided worshippers as they meditated on the paintings and followed the story of salvation, from picture to picture, around the church.

'we have heard and seen with our own eyes ...

we have watched and touched with our own hands' (1 John 1:1)

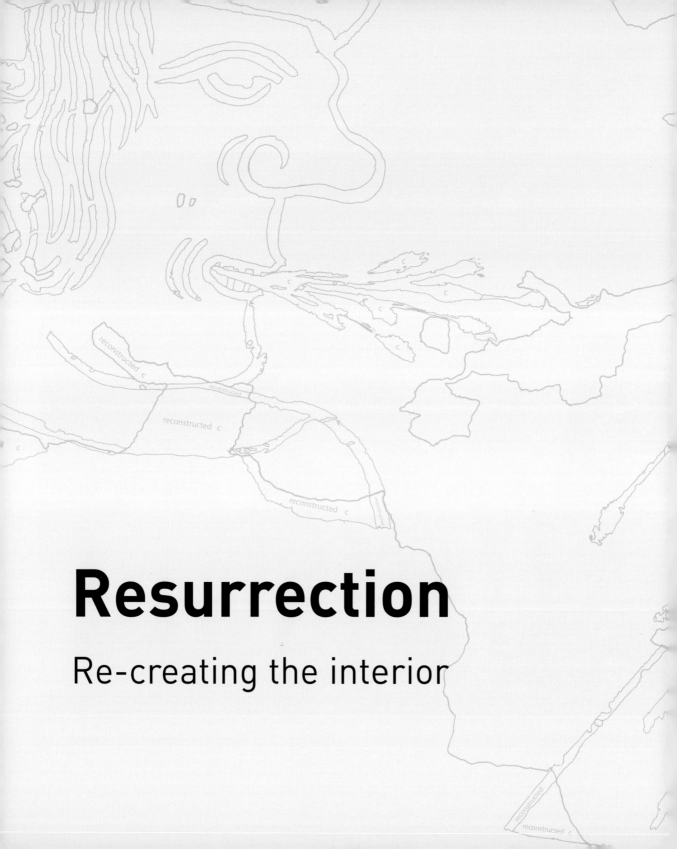

# Resurrection

Re-creating the interior

## The rood loft and wall paintings

The panelled front to the rood loft was formed as a blind arcading, divided into twelve compartments, based on examples found in the Marches. Many such panels, especially those found in churches in mid and north Wales, were pierced with decorative patterns. A few, like St Anno's in Llananno, were designed as 'niches' to display carved statues. Others had plain boards intended for painting with images of saints or angels. While a number of rood screens have survived in south Wales, their associated lofts have, almost without exception, been lost. However, churches in north Devon provide valuable examples. It is known that there were strong links between south Wales and north Devon in the Middle Ages, the two areas sharing a common seafaring tradition. Designs and materials from the west of England frequently crop up in churches in south Wales. As most of the rood screens in Glamorgan appear to have been built within the width of the chancel arch, there was little space available for painting images on the lower panels as was often done in north Devon. Surviving Glamorgan examples tended to be plain or decorated with carved linen-fold panels. Consequently, the emphasis moved to the front of the rood loft where arcaded panels, such as those re-created at St Teilo's, provided an ideal backcloth for portraying Biblical figures.

The Apostles were a popular subject in the late Middle Ages, and though Welsh examples have all been obliterated, they are frequently mentioned in the contemporary writings of the bards. The width of the nave, and consequently the width of the rood loft, lent itself to an arcade of twelve panels – ideal for portraying the twelve Apostles.

There were fairly set conventions in the way that the Apostles were depicted on painted screens. The commonest arrangement was the order set out in accordance with the Apostles' Creed, with each Apostle being associated with a particular portion of the Creed, which was generally shown as a piece of text below or alongside the Apostle in question. Generally, individual Apostles were identified by their symbols rather than their names. With an essentially illiterate population in areas such as Llandeilo Tal-y-bont, this would have made considerable sense.

In Wales, an alternative order has been identified, with Paul replacing Mathias. This arrangement was described by poets of the period such as Dafydd ap Gwilym and Iolo Goch, though he also lists Moses and David. It was therefore decided to base the line-up of Apostles on the arrangement described by the former, namely, from left to right: Simon, James (the Great), Andrew, Philip, John, Peter, Paul, Thomas, Bartholomew, Matthew, James (the Less) and Jude.

(Right) The pigments and techniques used to paint the screen and the Apostles were the same as those that would have been used during the late Middle Ages.

The designs for the various Apostles were based on surviving painted images from Devon, together with woodcuts from the period, in particular *The Mirrour of the Chyrche* by St Austin of Abingdon published by Wynkin de Worde in 1527.

There appeared to be two colour combinations that cropped up repeatedly, namely red and green, in alternating panels, or indigo and white. As many depictions of the Apostles showed them dressed in red or green robes, it was decided to go for a contrasting background, hence the choice of indigo and white. St Mary's church in Cheriton Bishop, north Devon, provides a parallel for the use of these colours as backgrounds.

(Following pages)
The Apostles:
Simon, James the
Great, Andrew,
Philip, John, Peter,
Paul, Thomas,
Bartholomew,
Matthew, James
and Jude.

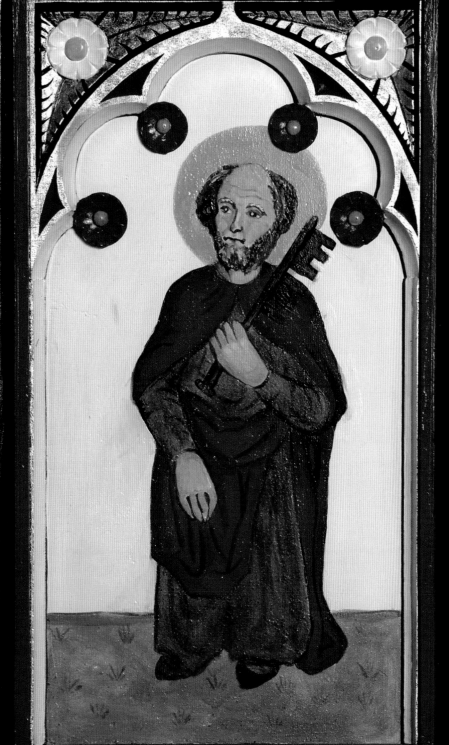

The choice of colours was limited to the range of pigments available to the artist at that period, the importance of the church and, perhaps most importantly, the funds available to pay for such work. Pigment, the raw material from which the paint is made, was ground with stand linseed oil on a flat slab with a flattened pestle-like grinder called a muller, to make a consistent hardwearing paint when dry. The pigments included lead white, lead tin yellow, indigo and true vermilion. Two pigments, madder and verdigris, are very transparent and better used as a glaze over another, denser paint layer. This is what was done with the red and white roses on the terminals of the cusps around the rood loft panels and also on the carved vine trails where the glazes were applied over gold and silver leaf. The one pigment not ground in oil was azurite, as it had to be kept in as large a particle size as possible to handle, in order for it to retain its colour. It was mixed with warm animal glue and applied immediately. Brushes were generally made by the artists themselves using squirrel or hogshair bound to wooden handles, or miniver (ermine) mounted in quills for very fine work, while oyster shells were often used as colour dishes to hold the pre-mixed pigments.

Gold leaf was often used to highlight carved mouldings and architectural details, as well as statues and even features such as haloes on some wall paintings. On the indigo-painted pilaster muntins between the panels of the rood loft are small stencilled

flowers, depicting pinks (or dianthus), in alternate silver and gold leaf. In the Middle Ages, pinks represented the Virgin Mary, and the flower was often used in this way in churches – another example that can be seen in St Mary's in Cheriton Bishop.

The original wall paintings at St Teilo's were executed *a secco*, by painting onto a dry plaster or limewash layer, as opposed to *a fresco*, where the painting is executed onto a fresh or wet plaster. With *buon fresco* ('true' fresco) paintings are executed using powder pigments, ground and mixed to a paste with water, which then bind with the wall surface through the carbonation of the lime in the lime

Applying gold leaf to decorative quatrefoils on the front of the rood screen.

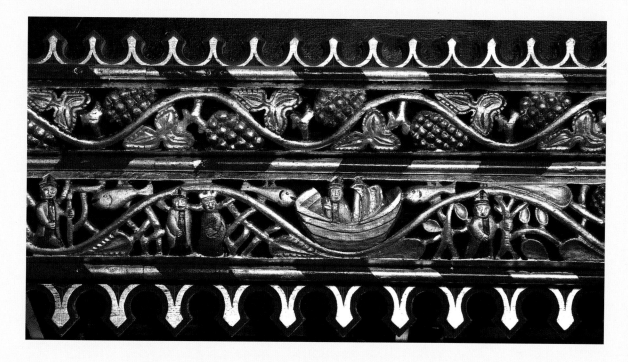

plaster. Lime putty (calcium hydroxide) sets through a process of carbonation, with the water element evaporating and atmospheric carbon dioxide being absorbed into the plaster to form calcium carbonate. During this process minute quantities of lime pass into the pigment layer and carbonate, thereby binding the pigments.

The wall paintings at St Teilo's were executed onto a thick limewash ground and in such cases the pigments normally require an additional binding medium. However, where thick freshly applied limewashes are present, it is arguable that the carbonation of the calcium hydroxide, which makes up the main component of this layer, would impart an element of fresco binding to the pigments. Such effects are sometimes referred to as *fresco-secco*, a somewhat confusing and contradictory term.

Colour, gold and silver leaf and glazing were used on the double vine-trail along the front of the rood loft, which illustrates scenes from Teilo's life.

The new wall paintings at St Teilo's have been executed using traditional *secco* painting techniques, in this case using a casein binder. Casein is the principle protein in milk and has been used since Egyptian times to make a form of tempera paint. Once the milk has been treated to produce an adhesive casein binding material, the casein glue can be diluted and mixed with traditional powder pigments. These are ground together to form a paste, which can then be applied in thin glazes. Several applications may be necessary to build up the colour, but the matte finish produced by this method is ideal for large mural subjects.

The powder pigments used were sourced from Clearwell Caves in the Forest of Dean. The Clearwell caves are among the earliest and one of the last producers of ochre, natural earth pigment, in the British Isles. Ochre is now thought to have been mined here for more than 7,000 years, since the Middle Stone Age. Until the 1930s, Forest of Dean mines had been famous for good quality, rich pigments, particularly shades of red and purple. Purple ochre is an unusual natural earth pigment; similar colours are usually only available in synthetic forms. Some of the Clearwell pigments have been mixed with other natural pigments obtained from L. Cornelissen & Son (established in London as an artists' colourman in 1855), in order to obtain close colour matches to the original wall paintings.

Many of the original wall paintings were set out using rough incised sketches made in the fresh limewash using a blunt point. This initial sketching is clearly seen in some of the surviving original fragments, and the soft edges of the incised lines show that the limewash was still wet and plastic (with a dry limewash layer one would have jagged, broken edges to the incised lines). The paintings were then executed quickly with free-flowing outline sketches, blocking-in of the main colours and final outlines added last.

The methods employed to reconstruct the murals were almost identical to the original techniques. The main exception was that the designs were first copied as outline cartoons and the images then transferred to the wall by 'pouncing'. Pouncing is a traditional technique, which can be identified on many Renaissance wall paintings. Here, the main outlines of the design (the 'cartoon') are pricked through using a needle or small spiked wheel to create a line of holes, and a small cloth bag containing fine powder pigment is patted over it to transfer dots of pigment, and thereby the image, through the holes.

The result, in this case, is a transferred cartoon image made up of a series of small red ochre dots. The unbound powder pigment is then overpainted, and mixed in, with the thin preliminary ochre outlines, sometimes referred to as *sinopia*. This term refers to the red oxide colour used for cartoons and under-drawing in *fresco* and *secco* painting and was described in the fifteenth century by Cennino Cennini in *Il Livro del Arte* as 'a

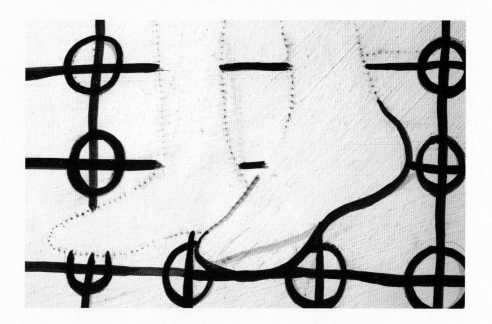

The dotted outline
of an image
transferred to the
plastered wall
surface by 'pouncing'.

natural colour known as sinoper, or porphyry, is red…'. Once the preliminary sketches have been finalised areas of flat or background colours are blocked in. Details and other colours are added layer by layer until the whole image is complete, when it can be given a final outline where necessary.

During the Medieval and Renaissance periods wall paintings in Britain were, for the most part, executed using a very basic palette of readily available and relatively inexpensive earth pigments – red and yellow ochres, lime white and carbon black. While the range of colours available to the artist included pigments such as red lead, white lead, vermilion, green earth, malachite, azurite and lapis lazuli (natural ultramarine), these pigments were often too expensive for the average rural community, and so their use tended to be limited to only the finest and grandest schemes, such as those that survive in some cathedrals and palaces.

The reconstruction of the wall paintings was carried out in a number of stages. A series of colour-matching tests were carried out and a simple palette of colours determined so that batches of colour could be made-up. Life-size photographic prints of the surviving wall paintings were located in their original positions on the walls of the reconstructed church. The outer borders and other architectural elements of the design

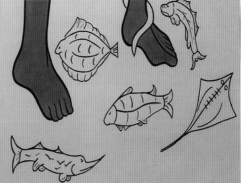

were copied and painted onto the recently limewashed walls. Within these areas the surviving figurative scenes were transferred as cartoons and subsequently painted-in. Initially, however, only the fragmentary 'islands' of surviving colour were painted, which were then used as the basis for reconstructing the missing areas.

In some cases the subject matter was clear, even though relatively little of the original remained, one of the best examples of this being the giant figure of St Christopher. Of the original, little more remained than the head of the saint turned to his right and facing towards a much smaller haloed figure, perched high on his shoulder. In the background was a small figure, with a lantern and holding a rosary, standing within an architectural setting. Combined with the traditional location, opposite the south door, these clues provided clear evidence that the scene depicted St Christopher, the patron saint of travellers. Having determined the style of the original artist, it was possible to look for other examples to provide source material on which to base a reconstruction of the missing areas. The main form for the figure of St Christopher was taken from a fine example at Llantwit Major; other elements were copied from another good depiction of the saint at Llanynys. The latter provided good source material for common decorative details often found in murals that depict the St Christopher story: in this case the fish swimming around the saint's massive legs, and features within the landscape such as the windmill.

Another such example was the Royal Arms on the south wall of the nave. Here, the quartered arms survived, surrounded by a garter and one of the two supporters (in this case, a dragon), but much of the heraldic detail and other information was missing. Fortunately, a late medieval example of a Royal Coat of Arms discovered some years

(Left) Details of the Royal Arms on the south wall of the nave.

(Right) Fish swimming around St Christopher's feet are featured in the painting on the north wall of the aisle.

ago at Cullacott farmhouse in Cornwall provided a good source of comparable material. In particular, this example was important because of the close stylistic similarities. There are important differences between wall paintings and other art forms, such as carved stone and wood, manuscript paintings or tapestries: while some of these may provide good examples of iconography from the right period, the stylistic variations can cause problems. Using the Cullacott Arms as the basis for this reconstruction, it was possible to overcome these problems and paint convincing lions passant and fleur-de-lys on the shield surrounded by the motto *honi soit qui mal y pense*. The Cullacott example also provided missing details on the dragon supporter, which in turn was used to reconstruct the lion on the opposite side.

The successful completion of the wall paintings will be a complex process, since not only does it require detailed investigation of the likely iconography, but also the sourcing of good comparative material. A wide range of source material must be found and studied to ensure that the new images are both iconographically and stylistically correct. As important, however, will be the ability of the modern painters to obtain the right 'feel' when executing the painting – and this requires an insight into the world of the original artist.

Cleaning the
Mocking of Christ in
a laboratory at
Cardiff University.
(1986)

Some of the main elements in place at the high altar including statues of St Teilo and the Madonna and child, the cross, candlesticks and riddel curtains.

## Furnishing the church

Nothing is known of the internal fixtures and fittings that once graced the interior of St Teilo's, and their lavishness would have depended on the scale of patronage, often manorial or monastic. However, we can get a good idea of what church furnishings were to be swept away by the Reformation from churchwardens' accounts documenting the sale of church plate, vestments and fittings, together with the more radical stripping of the church interior of its tabernacles and images. The pattern in Wales followed that in England – items thrown out of churches included vestments, crosses, paxes, censers, altar-cloths, rood cloths, basins, sacring bells, books and banners.

Of course, not all that glittered inside the late medieval church was made of gold. Many objects were made of base metals – brass, latten (a copper alloy containing zinc), gilt copper and gilt bronze. The altar, focal point for the celebration of Mass, would have required a number of sacred objects at various times, such as a chalice, pyx (a small container for the consecrated host), paten (the dish for the eucharistic wafer), cruets (small containers for water and wine) and a sanctus bell. In the absence of surviving furnishings and equipment from St Teilo's, it was decided to commission appropriate replicas based on objects that have survived from elsewhere in Wales or further afield.

The practice of placing a cross upon the altar during Mass appears to date from the thirteenth century, and while single-purpose crosses were made, most churches had a cross that could be both carried in procession and placed upon the altar. Even so, they were not vital if they duplicated the imagery of a retable or window glass, and they are rarely shown in manuscript illustrations. A processional cross was commissioned from Peter Shorer, a conservator and craftsman with a proven track record of producing accurate reproductions of archaeological artefacts, based on the incomplete fifteenth-century gilt copper-alloy cross from Llangynllo, now in the Museum's collections. The replica was made with copper electroform parts that were soldered together. Some of the missing elements were cast from surviving examples from elsewhere. The socketed stem used to attach the cross to the top of a staff was based on a surviving example from St Mary's Catholic Presbytery in Monmouth. A replacement for the missing evangelist roundel of Matthew was based on one from Monmouthshire. The figures of the Virgin Mary and St John, on crocketed branches either side of the cross, were rescaled versions of figures from Laleston in the Vale of Glamorgan and a site near Cardigan.

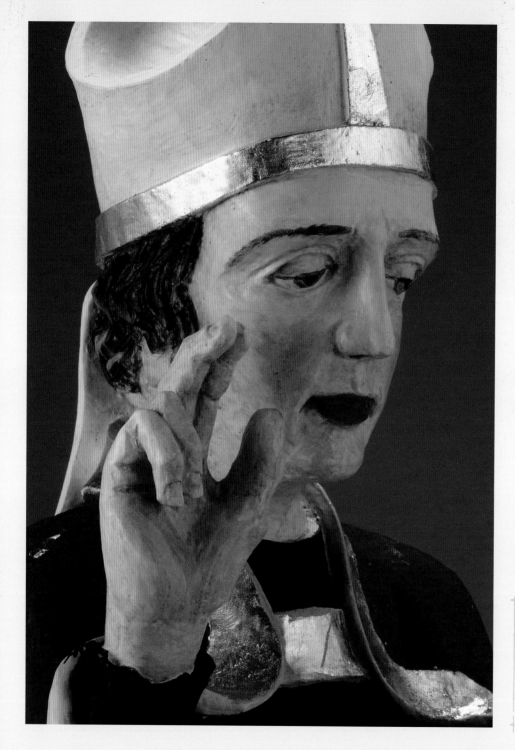

These statues of
St Teilo and the
Madonna and child,
carved by Emyr
Hughes, are based
on surviving
medieval examples
from Brittany.
They feature on
either side of the
high altar.

The replica
processional cross.

A small silver chalice was made by the Museum's blacksmith, Andrew Murphy, based on the plain mid-thirteenth-century silver chalice found in 1865/6 in the grave of a bishop, probably Richard de Carew (1256-80), at St David's Cathedral. This was chosen for its modest size and form, as St Teilo's may have been provided with something similar by one of its patrons.

The decision was made early on not to install permanent electric lighting, but to copy medieval conditions – relying on daylight and candles. While late medieval episcopal legislation stipulated that the only light required during Mass was a single wax taper, inventories suggest that most parish churches had two candles standing on the altar during all services – as shown by numerous manuscript illustrations. It was decided to install copies of late medieval latten candlesticks, based on the basic 'bunsen burner' type with cylindrical socket and drum base. Examples of such 'domestic' candlesticks are known from St Andrew's church in Wick, Tintern Abbey, Kenfig and Cardiff.

Medieval survivals illustrate more of the liturgical accessories that would have been familiar to the priest and congregation at St Teilo's. Examples include a fifteenth-century pax from Abergavenny, a thirteenth-century pewter cruet from White Castle, cheaper ceramic cruets such as one from Eglwys Gymyn, a sacring bell from Maenan Abbey in Gwynedd, and a copper-alloy censer from Gower.

According to canon law, it was usual to place three-dimensional images of the Virgin Mary and the patron saint of the parish church (or one representing its title) either side of the high altar and east window. As the east wall of the chancel was an early twentieth-century rebuild, the medieval architectural arrangement was not known. In keeping with the modest scale of the church, corbels were re-created to support effigies of Mary and St Teilo, behind which canopied niches were painted. Both figures were carved by Llangollen-born sculptor Emyr Hughes. The figure of the Virgin Mary was based largely on a figure of the Madonna and Child in the Musée de l'Evéche in Quimper, Britanny. Colour was added by Fleur Kelly, informed by studies of pigments on surviving sculpture like the fourteenth-century female saint from Mochdre. St Teilo is usually depicted robed as a bishop, riding on a stag. Medieval representations of St Teilo survive in Britanny, and include polychrome versions in wood at Abbaye Daoulas and Landeleau (the ancient oratory of St-Thélau/Teilo) and one in a fifteenth-century window in the St Teilo chapel in Plogonnec.

The rood, or cross, with the figure of Christ on it was an important focus of teaching and devotion in the medieval church. The Great Rood, a carved and painted crucifix, would have been flanked by the figures of the Blessed Virgin Mary and St John the Baptist, but on rare occasions they were replaced by the four Evangelists, or supplemented by additional figures. The figure of Christ on the now lost fifteenth-century rood loft at Brecon was flanked by the thieves, St John and the Virgin Mary, and the symbols of the four Evangelists. Emyr Hughes was commissioned to fashion a Christ for St Teilo's, based on the 1350-80 figure of Christ from Mochdre and archaeological reconstruction of its missing arms and legs. Carved in a bold, expressive style with deep relief for the torso, the Mochdre Christ would originally have been about 580 millimetres tall. Apart from Romanesque fragments from South Cerney, Gloucestershire (about 1125), only two

A rare late 14th-century statue of Christ found at Mochdre (left) was used as a pattern for the new carving (right).

The Great Rood, flanked by statues of the Blessed Virgin Mary and St John.

other polychrome wooden rood figures from Britain are known, namely the thirteenth-century figure from Kemeys Inferior and the late fifteenth-century carving from St Anthony's chapel in Cartmel Fell, Lancashire.

It is unclear how strictly colour schemes on figures were followed, as these could vary widely. White loincloths occur on surviving Continental figures and in manuscript illustrations. However, analysis of both the Kemeys and Mochdre figures has shown a prevailing red pigment, with traces of gilding, and this has been applied to the reconstruction.

(Left) The finished Rood, or statue of the crucified Christ.

As there are no surviving three-dimensional wooden images of the Virgin Mary or St John from England or Wales, images made of other materials, such as a fourteenth-century ivory diptych panel from Llandaff, were used to provide models for the specialist sculptors Jozeph Mesar and Jan Ferencik (working for Stuart Interiors of Somerset), who were commissioned to carve replicas for the rood loft.

The removal of many such images and rood-breaking, following the various instructions from 1547 to take them down, left a sense of outrage and violation in many communities, and some took it upon themselves to hide images rather than see them 'cut in pieces'. In Wales, disobedience to these policies was widespread but stopped short of outward resistance. Historical sources describe the post-Reformation survival of wooden images, hidden away like the Mochdre and Kemeys figures. Continuing reverence was recorded at Llanrwst church: 'Over the Timber Arch of the Chancell, neer the Rood Loft, lieth hid the ancient figure of the Crucifixion as bigg as the life. This, I suppose, is shewn to none but the curious, and rarely to them.'

In 1553, Mary succeeded Edward, and Catholic practices were revived until 1558, as reflected in churchwardens' accounts that record actions such as 'the making of the Rode', and 'for payntinge & gylldynge of the Rowde'. Further religious changes followed Elizabeth's succession in 1558. However, Catholic features appear to have survived in many Welsh churches well into Elizabeth's reign: as late as 1583, Bishop Middleton of St Davids felt it necessary to publish sets of critical injunctions banning images, altars and rood lofts. Many roods that survived the sixteenth-century reforms were later destroyed in the seventeenth century.

We don't know how long the original rood survived at St Teilo's. Creating, painting, gilding and re-erecting the rood figures for the church have vividly imitated fourteenth-century actions that were destined to repeat themselves, more than once.


## Altars, statues and fabrics

To the modern eye, the presence of so many altars might seem a little excessive. Particularly in recent times, we have grown accustomed to relatively simple interiors and the concentration on a single high altar in a parish church. Medieval churches and liturgy, however, encouraged a multiplication of altars as almost 'votive' objects associated with specific spiritual focus – centred for example on the passion of Jesus (the 'Jesus altar'), the Blessed Virgin Mary (the 'Lady altar') and the saints and angels. In this there may have been a continuity, to some degree, with the spirituality of pagan times. St Augustine of Canterbury had been instructed by Pope Gregory deliberately to retain pagan spiritual practices of longstanding that did not contradict and could be integrated into Christianity.

We know from the fabric of many Welsh churches, and in particular the survival of *piscinae* (where sacred vessels where washed) and aumbries (a recess in a wall where sacred vessels were stored), that they had a number of altars. There were probably five in St Teilo's church, possibly more. In addition to the principal altar in the chancel (the high altar), there was another at the end of the south aisle. This probably served the small south chapel, which was extended to form the aisle in the fifteenth century. Although this altar, like all the others in the church, had been removed or destroyed following the Reformation, its associated aumbrey still remained in the wall to its right. There is also a good deal of evidence from markings and the general carpentry of rood screens to show that altars were placed in front and to the side of them. Paintings and carvings that might have served as a reredos for such altars keep turning up, and in some cases, particularly in England, small stone side altars have survived, including some associated with the veneration of a local saint or relics. Patrishow church in Breconshire still retains its two altars in front of the rood screen, and similar features are known from Llanfilo and Pontfaen.

The evidence for rood screens has already been discussed, but their spiritual signifi-cance bears further reflection. Like the *iconostasis* in Eastern churches to this day, a similar screen decorated with icons that marks off the sanctuary, they served to emphasise the highly emotive and symbolic act that took place at the high altar during the celebration of the eucharist. The 're-presentation' of the sacrifice of Calvary was a key theme: one did not simply remember Christ's death, one was actually there – kneeling at the foot of the cross – somehow connected by a mystical bond with the event. All this was signified by the holiness of the sanctuary behind the screen, the many pictures of saints and angels (some often carved in the roof beams) and the great Rood, or Cross, depicting Christ's death presiding over everything.

In a similar way, the profusion of statues, carvings and wall paintings (for which we have growing evidence in Wales) should not be seen – as we tend to do now – as mere illustration. Primarily, a statue in a western church (like an icon in an eastern church) is a 'window' into the eternal, a place of meeting. Here you stand in the presence of Christ, the angels and saints, not because you worship an idol, of wood or stone, but because the Incarnation of God as Man in Jesus Christ made it possible to encounter God through the senses: 'we have heard and seen with our own eyes ... we have watched and touched with our own hands' (1 John 1:1). Or, as St Basil teaches (in his treatise *On the Holy Spirit*), the images we find in churches are a means of connection: the honour shown to them is believed to pass to the person they represent.

Many illustrations survive in printed missals and illuminated manuscripts that leave us in little doubt as to how altars, screens and statues were decorated and physically used. The Catholic community in Abergavenny, which continued to celebrate clandestine masses even when adherence to the Catholic faith was a punishable offence, preserved a number of pre-Reformation vestments and hangings. Embroidery (the so-called *opus anglicanum* for which Britain was famed) was used where it could be afforded. Again, the figures of Christ and the saints and angels were popular, as were images from nature such as flowers. This latter tendency is also manifested in versions of the hymn of Venantius Fortunatus that for hundreds of years accompanied the parish procession on Ascension Day: 'Daily the loveliness grows, adorned with the glory of blossom ... bright are the meadows with flowers.' This aspect of medieval culture is poorly understood by our 'minimalist' sensibilities – decoration was once a joyous thing, a celebration of creation.

Most altars were dressed in a way that is rarely seen today, though older people will remember that only fifty years ago it was very common (as a result of the revival of medieval liturgical fashions after Pugin and the Gothic Revival). Altars were hung with fine fabrics in front, and curtains at the sides. Sometimes they also had a 'dorsal' or back curtain, although more frequently a carved or painted reredos. Angels sometimes topped the curtain poles, and the altar itself was usually set on several steps. Nearby would be a place for washing vessels – the *piscina* already mentioned. Those in St Teilo's are based on surviving Welsh models. The pillar *piscina* to the right of the altar in the south aisle is a copy of a twelfth/thirteenth-century example at Oystermouth, while the wall *piscina* by the high altar is a copy from another Teilo church at Bishopston.

Canon law decreed that representations of Our Lady and the Patron Saint flanked the high altar, but the liturgical books allow us to be sure of many other requisites. The rood screen with its great cross was widespread across Europe before the Council of Trent in the mid-sixteenth century and reached great heights of elaboration. It was always pierced (the word chancel comes from the *cancella* or lattice-work of these screens or railings). After the Council, there was an emphasis on classical church models and a rejection of styles that could not prove antiquity, such as the rood screen. For the Sarum Use, (the celebration of Mass conducted according to the liturgical pattern established at Salisbury Cathedral) however, it was essential, marking the place of readings, the sacred space of the chancel and above all supporting the Rood, before which there were prescribed prayers each Sunday. Liturgical books give ample evi-

dence, as do churchwardens' accounts – as such work required a high degree of skill and investment, then as now. For the medieval church, however, the liturgy was an evolving, developing thing, and elaboration or richness was to be encouraged.

Looking around St Teilo's church, restored by painstaking craftsmanship after falling into ruin, some words from an ancient Orthodox prayer seem apposite: 'he has restored the sullied image to its ancient glory, filling it with the divine beauty'. This is what medieval Christians believed was achieved by Christ's coming to earth as a man, and it is no accident that their churches expressed this truth in concrete ways. They were witnesses to the Word made flesh, who had come close enough to mankind that his face could be seen and touched. In wood, glass, paint and stone they celebrated that closeness.

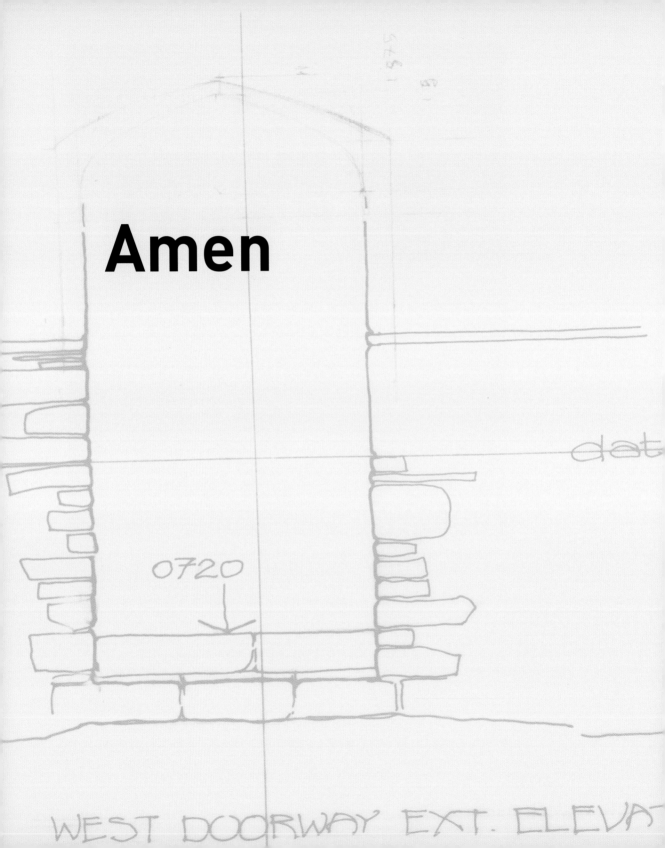

Amen

0720

dat

WEST DOORWAY EXT. ELEVA

# Bringing the church alive today

The careful, considered approach applied to the re-construction of St Teilo's is, upon entering the building, palpable. The senses are diverted at every turn by symbols, carvings, paintings, smells and ceremony: but for what purpose? Complex medieval theology and the church's role as a focus for the community it served are, ultimately, what shaped its structure and design. The colourful embellishments and decorations serve a world-view very different to our own, where the natural world served as inspiration and source of materials, income and food, as well as a reflection of the glory, and wrath, of God.

Entering and considering such a beguilingly simple building can be unsettling, as clues reveal themselves at an idiosyncratic rate. Due to the dazzling effect of the interior, and the exactitude to which it has been reconstructed, the distinction between 'new' and 'original' features is almost invisible. Replicas are displayed where originals did not survive, or are too fragile for the robust conditions inside the church. Examples of original sculptures, murals and ceramics are displayed in the galleries at St Fagans. Through this, we seek to explore the link between the scholarly discipline of conserving and displaying ancient objects with the altogether more lively process of designing, making and installing vibrant replicas. Where an almost tangible division exists in some critical circles between 'academic' and 'vernacular' art and architecture, St Teilo's church exposes and scrutinises where and how these schools of thought intersect.

Many visitors will experience a general reluctance to believe that any of the church's display is 'really Welsh', offering, instead, Italian, Greek, Moorish or even African examples of 'similar' paintings or places they have seen. The addition of a mural showing St George slaying the dragon might add to the confusion. The uncovering of a sizable, and cinematic, mural of the same scene in Llancarfan will hopefully corroborate and inform our own re-construction - as well as evoke a period where dragons were slithery demons that definitely did not come in cuddly-toy form. The Archbishop of Canterbury, Dr Rowan Williams, spoke at the opening of St Teilo's church about reclaiming a part of our past we ourselves are reluctant to believe existed. Other critics have praised the project for highlighting the contradictions and assumptions made by the modern eye, as well as for looking back on the way we used to see things.

From where it once stood on the marsh, St Teilo's church had long been an emblem of Pontarddulais and its surrounding communities. While our refurbished interior is an arresting departure from living memory, the lime-washed exterior appears today as it

does in countless paintings, souvenirs and decorated windows in Pontarddulais, where its likeness even graces the Town Mayor's chain. The relationship between the well-loved exterior, and the reconstructed razzle dazzle of the interior, then, was a potentially detached one, and our decision to reinstate the uncovered pre-Reformation murals was controversial.

Assumptions about the nature of Wales's religious built environment made some of our decisions appear, at best, frivolous, and at worst, downright gaudy. Sustained contact with the community at Pontarddulais helped us to reassure them that this was *their* history brought to life, rather than an intellectual or institutional flight of fancy. St Fagans brings to any building a means of uncovering its very silent history – one that is all too often shrouded in architecture, unruly repair work or vandalism.

Members of the Pontarddulais community still visit the church in its new location. This continuing interest culminates every year in a day of celebration. Together with members of the Wales and Marches Catholic History Society, parishioners from Pontarddulais hold a service at the Museum in honour of St Teilo on his saint's day, the ninth of February.

General visitors have also been invited to observe the building's re-construction – many fondly remembering the piles of numbered stones they first encountered in 1997 as they would a child in its infancy. In encouraging the public to approach and talk to the craftsmen, we have engaged with a completely new audience. Their response to the handiwork is one of genuine, lively fascination rather than nostalgia for familiar, 'lost' disciplines. We found that visitors would come back again and again to see, for example, a mural being traced, measured, pounced and painted. Though it is the interpreter's job to make religion and society in the 1520s as attractive and interesting a topic as possible, one must concede that the effect of a hand-made timber-framed roof or carefully decorated screen can sometimes be more convincing.

Officially opened at St Fagans in 2007, St Teilo's church has been taken back in time around ten years for every mile it travelled along the M4 from Pontarddulais to Cardiff. It now responds to its new setting, though the faint murmur of the motorway is still audible through the trees – a memory, perhaps, of its original location by Junction 48. Media coverage has brought new visitors in their tens of thousands, and we are now faced with how best to look after it and use it.

This is believed to be the only stone-built church in Europe to have been re-erected and refurbished to its medieval appearance, and we hope that it will become a space to explore the role of worship through the ages, and consequently develop into a 'social centre' again. The building will certainly act as a key: anyone who has seen St Teilo's in all its glory can now take it with them to the wealth of religious heritage sites across Wales. The visitor can, as we have done, imaginatively re-build, from near-ruin, a structure whose colour and effect have long faded – where all that remains is 'that feeling' we encounter in sacred spaces.

Deceptively simple in its appearance, the church is conceptually more complex than most other buildings at St Fagans. The richness of the symbolic decoration was originally meant to last a generation of Sundays spent looking, learning and meditating. The concept of complexity-into-simplicity that is so prevalent in the medieval Christian cosmology is also visible in St Teilo's – complementing the natural world, and therefore the worshipper's place in it. Half an hour's visit cannot even begin to unravel the nature of the building. Fortunately, as people are drawn back to St Teilo's time and time again, they not only chart its progress and meaning, but also become a part of it.

## A personal footnote

At the end of his book *Beautiful Wales*, published in 1905, the poet Edward Thomas describes the marshes at the estuary of the River Loughor and tells of '...a little desolate white church and white-walled graveyard.' Although he neither names the river nor the church, anyone who knows the area will immediately recognise both. The church is the subject of this book, and if Thomas felt a poetic desolation in 1905, eighty years later that desolation had become visible due to the ravages of time and climate, in spite of valiant efforts to maintain the building. Of course in 1905, the church had already ceased to be the parish church (the new St Teilo's had been granted that title in 1851), and had only been used for worship a few times every year.

The process of dismantling the church in 1985 and 1986 was painful for many in the locality. In spite of its remoteness and decay, parishioners still remembered worshipping there. It was a focus for communal gatherings, family walks on sunny Sunday evenings, picnics and lovers' trysts. It was (and remains still) an icon for the community, appearing on the insignia of Pontarddulais Town Council and several other organizations. Homes in the area display plates, mugs, cups, medallions, cards and other mementos featuring its immediately recognisable shape, and many exhibit drawings or paintings of *Yr Hen Eglwys* ('the old church') in a variety of styles and by a profusion of artists, both amateur and professional, from the past one hundred years and more.

It was a privilege for me to witness the whole process of careful investigation prior to the removal of the layers of whitewash, and to be allowed, under supervision, to help. What a thrill it was to be there when the two remnants of the Lord's Prayer in Welsh were uncovered! The revealing of layers of painted inscriptions and pictures, their recording and salvaging, and the delight at each fresh revelation, with accompanying attempts at initial classification, still resonates with excitement. Then the deliberate and precise disassembling of the structure, and the seemingly interminable delay before the removal of the stones to their new site. Let's not use the journalistic cliché 'stone by stone', conjuring images of a line of St Fagans' workers stretching along the M4 and back like leaf-cutter ants, each with a stone on its back!

The eventual painstaking reconstruction and re-creation of the church as it might have looked about 1530 has provided a challenge. It was important to reassure those who remembered the building decked internally in its nineteenth-century form, that this rather alien display of late medieval flamboyance was as much part of our rich and varied heritage in Wales as the more austere internal arrangement of Capel Pen-rhiw, the small Unitarian chapel also re-erected at the Museum. This is a history Wales is rediscovering, in her own religious art and literature of the Middle Ages, reminding us that we belong to a rich European heritage.

However, just as some mistakenly believe that the church can only have been as it was in its final 1810 form, we must not think the same of the 1530 embodiment. From 1530, history can take us both backwards and forwards, and the bringing of the church to St Fagans has shown that the 'space' used for Christian worship changes from generation to generation. The austerity of 'Celtic' Christianity, with the call of the early missionary saints of western Britain; the devotion of the changing years of the medieval period coupled with the ravages of plagues and battles for nationhood; the translating of the Bible and Prayer-book into Welsh; the relationship of the Established Church with Welsh expressions of religious non-conformity; the disestablishment of the Church in Wales in 1920 and finally the response of the churches in Wales to a pluralist and secular culture – the church has constantly adapted to different emphases in the expression of Christian worship. It has managed, through the succession of generations of worshippers, to be part of the rich social history of the parish it serves.

With 'the old church' now rebuilt at St Fagans, there is a feeling of pride and delight among the people of Pontarddulais and district that our local treasure is now recognised as a national treasure, which Wales is sharing with the world. Although the church Edward Thomas saw in 1905 is no longer on the banks of the River Loughor, the *Llan* that bears Teilo's name remains, and Teilo's contemporary family continues to gather in his, and his Lord's, name.

'...a little desolate white church and white-walled graveyard'

(Edward Thomas, 1905)

# Contributors

**Ken Brassil MA, MSc**
Archaeology/History Education Officer, Amgueddfa Cymru – National Museum Wales. Undertook archaeological excavations at site of St Teilo's church, Llandeilo Tal-y-bont.

**Robert Child BSc, FIIC, FSA**
Head of Conservation at Amgueddfa Cymru – National Museum Wales. Involved in uncovering the wall paintings at St Teilo's church.

**Daveth H. Frost BSc, Cert Theol.**
Principal of Holy Cross Catholic College, Bury, formerly Acting Principal of St David's Catholic College, Cardiff and Chairman of 1520 Group, Wales and Marches Catholic History Society.

**Madeleine Gray PhD**
Senior Lecturer in History in the University of Wales, Newport and one of the editors of the Gwent County History. Author of *Images of Piety*, dealing with the iconography of late medieval religion in Wales.

**Sara Huws BA**
Studied History of Art & Architecture at Emanuel College, Cambridge. Education Interpreter at St Teilo's church.

**Fleur Kelly**
Freelance artist specialising in painting on panel. Trained under Leonetto Tintori. Conservator at the Pitti Palace, Florence. Has worked on numerous commissions for churches, private clients and museums.

**Rev. John Morgan-Guy BA, PhD, FRHistS**
Currently Arts & Humanities Research
Council Research Fellow in the Department
of Theology and Religious Studies,
University of Wales, Lampeter and Honorary
Research Fellow of the University.

**Gerallt D. Nash BSc, BArch, FSA**
Graduate of the Welsh School of Architecture,
Cardiff. Senior Curator, Historic Buildings at
Amgueddfa Cymru – National Museum Wales
and Project Leader on the St Teilo's church
project.

**Thomas Organ ACR**
Trained in the conservation of medieval wall
paintings at Canterbury Cathedral before
studying mural conservation in Italy. Since 1991,
has run The Wall Paintings Workshop – an
independent team of conservators and
conservation consultants.

**Rev. Anthony J. Parkinson MA, FSA**
Formerly Investigator for the Royal Commission
on the Ancient Monuments of Wales,
responsible for recording historic buildings
under threat, and for initiating the Commission's
database of wall paintings in churches.

**Mark Redknap BA, PhD, MIFA, FSA**
Graduate of the Institute of Archaeology,
University of London. Curator of
Medieval & Later Archaeology at Amgueddfa
Cymru – National Museum Wales. Co-author
with John M. Lewis of volume one of the *Corpus
of Early Medieval Inscribed Stones and Stone
Sculpture in Wales*.

**Andrew Renton BA, PGCE, AMA**
Trained as a classicist at Oxford University and
taught for several years before
becoming a curator at National Museums
Liverpool in 1993. Head of Applied Art at
Amgueddfa Cymru – National Museum Wales,
responsible for its collections of ceramics, silver
and other applied art from the Renaissance to
the present day.

**Rev. John Walters**
Vicar of Llandeilo Tal-y-bont from 1983;
the parish retains its ancient name, and
is now mainly centred on the town of
Pontarddulais, with the two churches St Teilo's
and St Michael's.

**David Watkinson MSc, FIIC, ACR, FSA**
Graduate in conservation at University College
London and Cardiff University. Currently Reader
in Conservation at Cardiff University responsible
for BSc and MSc artefact conservation courses
and care of collections.

**Eurwyn Wiliam MA, PhD, FSA**
Graduate in archaeology at Cardiff University
and vernacular architecture at Manchester
University. Director of Collections & Research
and Deputy Director General of Amgueddfa
Cymru – National Museum Wales.

# Reference

## Further reading

Binski, Paul *Medieval Craftsmen: painters*, British Museum Press (1991)

Cartwright, Jane (ed.) *Celtic Hagiography and Saints' Cults*, University of Wales Press (2003)

Child, Mark *Discovering Church Architecture: a glossary of terms*, Shire Publications (1984)

Child, Mark *Discovering Churches and Churchyards*, Shire Publications (2007)

Coldstream, Nicola *Medieval Craftsmen: masons and sculptors*, British Museum Press (1991)

Coldstream, Nicola *Builders & Decorators: Medieval craftsmen in Wales*, Cadw Publications (2008)

Duffy, Eamon *The Stripping of the Altars: traditional religion in England 1400-1580*, Yale University Press (1992)

Evans, E. Lewis (ed.) Translated by Ivor Griffiths *The History of Pontardulais*, (published privately, copies available for reference in Swansea Libraries) (1985)

Gray, Madeleine *Images of Piety: the iconography of traditional religion in late medieval Wales*, Archaeopress (2001)

Hislop, Malcolm *Medieval Masons*, Shire Publications (2000)

Holmes, George (ed.) *The Oxford Illustrated History of Medieval Europe*, Oxford University Press (2001)

Hughes, T.J. *Wales's Best One Hundred Churches*, Seren (2006)

Jenkins, Simon *Wales: churches, houses, castles*, Penguin (2008)

Lord, Peter *The Visual Culture of Wales: medieval vision*, University of Wales Press (2003)

Marks, Richard *Stained Glass in England during the Middle Ages*, Routledge (1993)

Robinson, John M. *Treasures of the English Churches*, Sinclair-Stevenson (1995)

Robinson, David M. *The Cistercians in Wales: architecture and archaeology 1130-1540*, Oxbow Books (2006)

Rosewell, Roger *Medieval Wall Paintings in English and Welsh Churches*, The Boydell Press (2008)

Rouse, E. Clive *Medieval Wall Paintings*, Shire Publications (1991)

Walker, David (ed.) *A History of the Church in Wales*, Church in Wales Publications (1976)

Walker, David *Medieval Wales*, Cambridge University Press (1990)

Wheeler, Richard *Medieval Church Screens of the Southern Marches*, Logaston Press (2006)

Williams, David H. *The Welsh Cistercians*, Gracewing (2001)

Williams, Glanmor *Renewal and Reformation – Wales c.1415-1642*, Oxford University Press (1987)

Williams, Glanmor *Wales and the Reformation*, University of Wales Press (1997)

Williams, Glanmor; Jacob, William; Yates, Nigel; Knight, Frances *The Welsh Church from Reformation to Disestablishment 1603-1920*, University of Wales Press (2007)

# Glossary

**Auger**
A hand-held bit used for boring holes vertically into the ground to remove samples of sediment or rock.

**Aumbry**
A recess in a church wall where sacred vessels are stored.

**Chantries**
Privately endowed chapels inside churches, where the priest would say prayers for the deceased.

**Chancel**
The part of the church east of the nave, containing the high altar. It is often separated by a screen, and sometimes known as the sanctuary or choir.

**Corbel**
A block that protrudes from a wall to support elements like arches, beams or statues.

**Datum line**
A horizontal or vertical line drawn through or around a building, and then used as a central reference from which to take vertical and horizontal measurements.

**Motte and bailey**
The motte is an earth mound upon which a small medieval castle would have been built. The bailey is an adjoining but separately defined enclosure.

**Nave**
The main body of the church, to the west of the chancel (see above).

**Papal bull**
A charter issued by a pope. The term 'bull' comes from 'bulla', which was the metal seal that was tied through slits in the document.

**Putlog**
The horizontal parts, or cross-timbers, of a scaffold structure. Putlog holes are the small, square holes formed in masonry walls, into which the timbers were placed and secured.

**Rood**
A carved depiction of Christ on the cross.

**Squint**
A hole cut through a wall to enable the high altar to be viewed from another part of a church.

**Transept**
An extension to a church, to the south and/or north, often creating a cruciform plan.

## Plan of the church

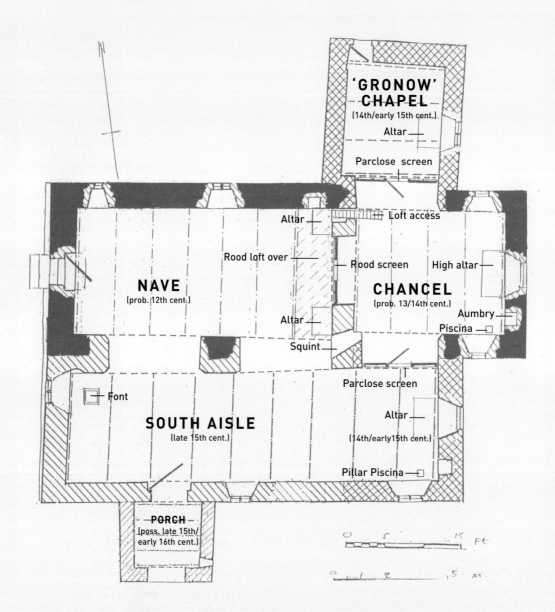

'GRONOW' CHAPEL
(14th/early 15th cent.)

Altar

Parclose screen

Loft access

Altar

Rood loft over

Rood screen

High altar

NAVE
(prob. 12th cent.)

CHANCEL
(prob. 13/14th cent.)

Altar

Aumbry

Piscina

Squint

Parclose screen

Font

Altar

SOUTH AISLE
(late 15th cent.)

(14th/early15th cent.)

Pillar Piscina

PORCH
(poss. late 15th/
early 16th cent.)

## Other Teilo churches in south Wales

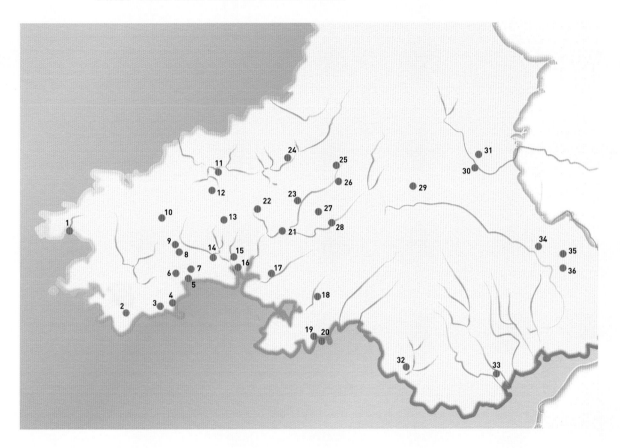

1. St Elvis
2. Stackpole
3. *Eglwys Guinniou*
4. Penally
5. Amroth
6. Ludchurch
7. Crunwear
8. Crinow
9. Llandeilo Llwyn Gaidan
10. Llandeilo Llwydarth
11. Maenordeifi
12. Cilrhedyn
13. Trelech
14. Llanddowror
15. Llandeilo Abercywyn
16. Llandeilo Pentywyn
17. Capel Teilo
18. Llandeilo Tal-y-bont
19. Bishopston
20. Caswell
21. Llandeilo Rhwnws
22. Llanpumsaint
23. Brechfa
24. Llanfechan
25. Caio
26. Capel Teilo
27. Ffynnon Teilo
28. Llandeilo Fawr
29. Llandeilo'r Fan
30. Crickadarn
31. Llandeilo Graban
32. Merthyr Mawr
33. Llandaff
34. Llandeilo Pertholey
35. Llandeilo Gresynni
36. Llan-arth

# Welsh places noted in the book

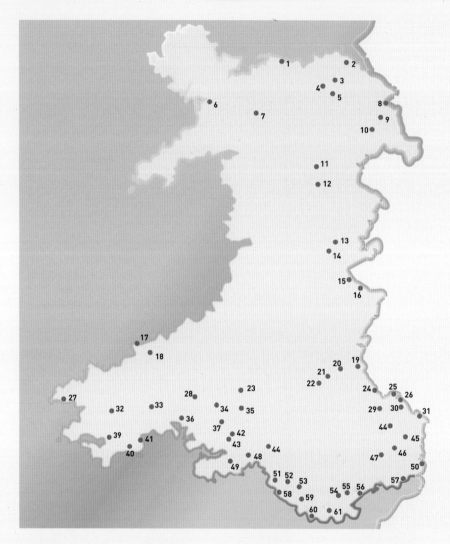

| | | | |
|---|---|---|---|
| 1 Llanelian-yn-Rhos | 17 St Dogmaels | 32 Slebech | 48 Swansea |
| 2 Holywell | 18 Cilgerran | 33 Whitland | 49 Bishopston |
| 3 Llandyrnog | 19 Llanelieu | 34 Pontfaen | 50 Mathern |
| 4 Llanrhaeadr | 20 Llanfilo Llanfilo | 35 Llandybie | 51 Kenfig |
| 5 Llanynys | 21 Brecon | 36 Llanstephan | 52 Laleston |
| 6 Caernarfon | 22 Llanfaes | 37 Derwydd | 53 Colwinston |
| 7 Dolwyddelan | 23 Llandeilo Fawr | 38 Llanfair Cilgedin | 54 Peterston super Ely |
| 8 Gresford | 24 Patrishow | 39 Cosheston | 55 St Fagans |
| 9 Wrexham | 25 Llangattock Lingoed | **40 Penally** | **56 Cardiff/Llandaff** |
| 10 Ruabon | 26 Skenfrith | 41 Tenby | 57 Kemeys Inferior |
| 11 Pennant Melangell | 27 St Davids | **42 Pontarddulais** | 58 Newton Nottage |
| 12 Llanwddyn | 28 Carmarthen | **43 Llandeilo Tal-y-bont** | 59 Wick |
| 13 Newtown | 29 Llangar | 44 Neath | 60 Llantwit major |
| 14 Mochdre | 29 Abergavenny | 45 Gwernesney | 61 Llancarfan |
| 15 Llananno | 30 Llantilio Crossenny | 46 Llangybi | |
| 16 Llangynllo | 31 Monmouth | 47 Llantarnam | |